Grace Notes

FIVE-MINUTE INSPIRATIONAL DEVOTIONALS FOR
THE CHURCH CHOIR,
MUSICIANS, AND FRIENDS OF MUSIC

Grace Notes

FIVE-MINUTE INSPIRATIONAL DEVOTIONALS FOR
THE CHURCH CHOIR,
MUSICIANS, AND FRIENDS OF MUSIC

Marlene Jenkins Cooper

Songs of Judah Publishing, LLC
Philadelphia, PA

Book Layout © 2015 BookDesignTemplates.com

Grace Notes/ Marlene Jenkins Cooper -- 1st ed.

Publisher: Songs of Judah Publishing, LLC

ISBN: 978-0-9961227-7-1

1. Devotional 2. Choir 3. Spiritual Growth 4. Christian Living

First Edition

Printed in United States of America

DEDICATION

To My Mother, Dorothy Jenkins

Who introduced me to Jesus, music, hymns, the piano and organ, and serving Jesus

Table of Contents

Foreword   xi
Acknowledgements   xv
Introduction   xvii
Directions For The Devotional Leader   xviii

Devotional One   Grace   2
Devotional Two   Walk   4
Devotional Three   Walk With Me   6
Devotional Four   Seek   8
Devotional Five   Praise   10
Devotional Six   Sing   12
Devotional Seven   Risen   14
Devotional Eight   Knees   16
Devotional Nine   Clouds   18
Devotional Ten   Lamb of God   20
Devotional Eleven   Hills   22
Devotional Twelve   Pastures   24
Devotional Thirteen   Blessings   26
Devotional Fourteen   Hallelujah   28
Devotional Fifteen   Glory   30
Devotional Sixteen   Glory and Honor   32
Devotional Seventeen   Look   34
Devotional Eighteen   Clouds   36
Devotional Nineteen   And They Sang   38
Devotional Twenty   Hands   40
Devotional Twenty-one   Salt   42
Devotional Twenty-two   Cast   44
Devotional Twenty-three Power   46
Devotional Twenty-four Presence   48
Devotional Twenty-five Late   50
Devotional Twenty-six   Joy   52
Devotional Twenty-seven Angels   54

Devotional Twenty-eight	Faithfulness	56
Devotional Twenty-nine	Care	58
Devotional Thirty	Miracle	60
Devotional Thirty-one	Tribulation	62
Devotional Thirty-two	Praise	64
Devotional Thirty-three	All	66
Devotional Thirty-four	Jesus	68
Devotional Thirty-five	Lift	70
Devotional Thirty-six	Fear Not	72
Devotional Thirty-seven	Fear	74
Devotional Thirty-eight	Day	76
Devotional Thirty-nine	Light	78
Devotional Forty	King	80
Devotional Forty-one	Refuge	82
Devotional Forty-two	Alone	84
Devotional Forty-three	Love	86
Devotional Forty-four	Ready	88
Devotional Forty-five	Drink / Thirst	90
Devotional Forty-six	Hope	92
Devotional Forty-seven	Lamp	94
Devotional Forty-eight	Blood	96
Devotional Forty-nine	Adore	98
Devotional Fifty	Mighty	100
Devotional Fifty-one	Lost	102
Devotional Fifty-two	Morning	104
Devotional Fifty-three	Heaven	106
Devotional Fifty-four	Love	108
Devotional Fifty-five	Crown	110
Devotional Fifty-six	Magnify	112
Devotional Fifty-seven	Mercy	114
Devotional Fifty-eight	Serve	116
Devotional Fifty-nine	Presence	118
Devotional Sixty	Victory	120
Devotional Sixty-one	Shepherd	122
Devotional Sixty-two	New	124
Devotional Sixty-three	Communion	126

Devotional Sixty-four	Cross	128
Devotional Sixty-five	Sin	130
Devotional Sixty-six	Holy	132
Devotional Sixty-seven	Nobody	134
Devotional Sixty-eight	Testimony	136
Devotional Sixty-nine	Emmanuel	138
Devotional Seventy	Teach	140
Devotional Seventy-one	Hope	142
Devotional Seventy-two	Wonderful	144
Devotional Seventy-three	Anything	146
Devotional Seventy-four	Supply	148
Devotional Seventy-five	Greater	150
Devotional Seventy-six	Cross	152
Devotional Seventy-seven	Satisfy	154
Devotional Seventy-eight	Rock	156
Devotional Seventy-nine	Listen	158
Devotional Eighty	Temptation	160
Devotional Eighty-one	Promise	162
Devotional Eighty-two	Call	164
Devotional Eighty-three	Lift	166
Devotional Eighty-four	Peace	168
Devotional Eighty-five	Joy	170
Devotional Eighty-six	Truth	172
Devotional Eighty-seven	Name	174
Devotional Eighty-eight	Rejoice	176
Devotional Eighty-nine	Mighty	178
Devotional Ninety	Cross	180
Devotional Ninety-one	Mighty	182
Devotional Ninety-two	Voice	184
Devotional Ninety-three	Refuge	186
Devotional Ninety-four	Worship	188
Devotional Ninety-five	Battle	190
Devotional Ninety-six	Touch	192
Devotional Ninety-seven	Free	194
Devotional Ninety-eight	Light	196
Devotional Ninety-nine	Glory	198

Devotional One Hundred   Valley   200

Invitation to Salvation   202
Sinner's Prayer   205
About the Author   207
Devotional Theme Index   209
Devotional Scripture Index   213

FOREWORD

Beloved music educator, musician, and author Marlene Cooper, follows her book *While in the Valley* with St. Paul's encouragement in her new book, *Grace Notes: Five Minute Inspirational Devotionals For The Church Choir, Musicians, and Friends of Music* (Colossians 3:16). Marlene Cooper follows St. Paul's words by encouraging and inciting musicians and choir members to include a devotional in their personal time and in their rehearsals. *Grace Notes* addresses church choir members, musicians, and friends of music.

Marlene Cooper realizes that, along with the Bible, music cleanses, aligns, and pampers the soul for the greater actualization and realization of personal devotion and regular choir rehearsals. Marlene Cooper's book *Grace Notes* realizes that the most valiant and impactful musicians and choirs for God have been the musicians and choirs who have had prominent devotional lives. Thus the most impactful musicians and choirs never resist the urge to incorporate devotional study, music, and prayer, either before, during, or after rehearsals.

A devotional of reflection, prayers to God, and music, *Grace Notes* is a spa-bath of Living Water. Thus, this new publication celebrates each rehearsal and personal devotion with the Word, prayer, and song, celebrating the unfailing Love of God, and it is especially for busy church musicians, bands, music tours, worship teams, worship leaders, praise teams, pianist and organist, and choir members.

Marlene Cooper realizes the ultimate test of our understanding, love, and obedience to God will be enhanced by the regular rehearsal review and reading of *Grace Notes*. To illustrate this belief, Marlene Cooper provides 100 devotionals to the reader. Please read and use *Grace Notes'* 100 devotionals in rehearsal and in personal devotions. A review of these pages will regularly help musicians and choir members increase their confidence in God, in choir rehearsal warm-ups and personal devotion, and keener recognition of the power of the living God.

Grace Notes challenges the musician and choir who believe that the rehearsal doesn't "take all that." But something of great importance happens when the musician and choir gathers at Jesus' feet in devotion, song and prayer...the heart beholds the everlasting mystery of God's Love. While in rehearsal, some musicians and choir members may be tired, weary, and worn. Thus, for these members, there may not be a song in their heart. Through

Marlene's book, the devotional enables our mouths and hearts to sing anyway!

Finally, as musicians and members of choirs, in rehearsals, our mouths may sing and our heads mentally grasp, but only our hearts can revere and worship through devotional time, prayer and song adoration.

Philip Bingham
Minister of Music - Emeritus
Concord Baptist Church of Christ
Brooklyn, NY

ACKNOWLEDGMENTS

First and foremost, I would like to thank God for helping me write this devotional. As I wrote, I listened and heard the voice of the Lord during my quiet times, which in turn helped me write this devotional. I could never have done this project without the faith I have in you.

I would like to express my gratitude to the church musicians, choristers, friends, and my family who provided support and assisted in the beta reading and design of this devotional. I am grateful to the many pastors who allowed me to walk in my purpose as I ministered with their choirs and congregations. To all the church choirs that I have ministered with in music ministry, I want to say how grateful I am for the opportunity. Thanks to everyone who has encouraged me in music ministry.

Above all, I want to thank my children, Joy and Mark, who went to countless choir rehearsals, church services, and concerts. They supported and encouraged me in spite of all the time it took me away from them. Many thanks to my mom, dad, and siblings, who encouraged me in music ministry by their support. Thanks everyone!

INTRODUCTION

Grace Notes originated out of my need for such a book to read during my church choir rehearsals. At every rehearsal, I wanted a short devotional to share with the choir before we started rehearsing and learning new music. I wanted the devotional to align itself with the theme and focus of the songs we would rehearse. Planning each week for the devotional warm-up and the music for choir rehearsal was time consuming. It was my desire for the choir and I to have a musical, spiritual, and worship experience during our time together. I needed a choral devotional book!

During this time in my life, the Lord was giving me two to three key spiritual vocabulary words each month as I read the Bible in my personal devotions. I decided to use these key words as a focus for writing a devotional book for choirs and personal devotion. My prayer is that your music ministry and personal devotions will benefit from the time spent together in the Word of God, prayer, and song. Enjoy!

"Sing"erly,

Marlene Jenkins Cooper

Directions for the Devotional Leader

Purpose

The purpose of *Grace Notes* is to give the church choir and the musicians a time to corporately come together to read scripture, reflect, pray, and sing before or after rehearsing and learning music. *Grace Notes* also fosters time alone with God during personal devotions.

Uses for *Grace Notes*

Each devotional requires five minutes of the rehearsal time and can be before or after rehearsal or at another designated time. The choir devotional could be thought of as a prelude/postlude to the rehearsal. Each devotional begins with scripture, then offers a reflection and a brief prayer, and closes with a song from the list given at the end of the devotional, or from the choir's repertoire.

The initial scripture(s) are aligned with the theme or focus of the devotional. The reflection also correlates with the theme of the devotion. Four songs have been chosen to go along with each theme. Choose one song at the conclusion of the devotional to sing together. Other options include listening to a recording or view a YouTube video of the chosen song. Feel free to sing or listen to the entire song, only the chorus, one particular verse, or any other song in the choir's repertoire that is not listed in the book. Therefore, each devotional is a complete unit that explores a particular idea or theme. Since the choristers may want to comment or ask questions during the devotional time together, please allow for interaction. However, be mindful of the time and keep the rehearsal time on course. A five-minute timer or a personal timekeeper is a great tool to help with time management.

The songs listed in *Grace Notes* represent different genres of Christian music, from Negro Spiritual to anthems. The devotional leader can be anyone—the choir director, a choir member, and leadership of the church, or any praise team or band member, or choir chaplain. If you are using this book with more than one music group, it may be helpful to notate the date each devotional is used, along with the name of the music group. Also, feel free to write in the margins additional thoughts, comments, and song titles that will enhance the devotional for the music group. In addition, anyone involved in the music ministry of the church, Christian music group, or friend of church music may also want to use this book for their personal devotional time. May God be praised!

GRACE NOTES

Five-Minute

Inspirational Devotionals

For The Church Choir,

Musicians,

and

Friends of Music

Grace

2 Corinthians 12:9

"And he said unto me, My grace is sufficient for thee: for my strength is made perfect in weakness. Most gladly therefore will I rather glory in my infirmities, that the power of Christ may rest upon me."

When the word *grace* is spoken, what comes to mind? Perhaps this scripture or the definition of the word *grace*, which is God's unmerited favor. Some call to mind the scriptures in Ephesians 2:8-9, which states, "For by grace are ye saved through faith; and that not of yourselves: it is the gift of God: Not of works, lest any man should boast." God's favor is a benefit we did not merit. God's grace is unmatchable. Today we praise and thank God for His favor and grace. Without His grace, where would we be? We would be lost, because we are saved only by His grace.

Some people mix up the definitions of grace and mercy. These words are often used interchangeably, but grace and mercy do not mean the same thing. God's mercy means not receiving what we deserve. God's grace means receiving His unmerited, undeserved favor and blessings.

Let's praise God for His grace, which covers a multitude of sins, errors, and transgressions.

Dear Lord, We are ever so grateful for the grace, your unmerited favor, which you bestow upon us. We thank you that you loved us enough to save us from our sins and give us eternal life. O God Our Father, we thank you for your grace, which is sufficient and more than enough for each one of us. Thank you Lord for inspiring the Apostle Paul to write these words, "My grace is sufficient for thee: for my strength is made perfect in weakness" (2 Corinthians 12:9). Thank you, dear Father. Amen.

Songs Related to Grace:

1. Grace Greater Than Our Sin - Julia H. Johnston
                                    Daniel B. Towner
2. Amazing Grace - John Newton
3. God's Grace - Luther Barnes
4. Wonderful Grace of Jesus - Haldor Lillenas

Walk

Psalm 23:4

"Even though I walk through the valley of the shadow of death, I will fear no evil, for you are with me."

The Negro Spiritual, "I Want Jesus to Walk with Me," speaks of having the Lord walk with us during our difficult journeys. Another Negro Spiritual, entitled "Guide My Feet," asks Jesus for His help while running the race of life. The Negro slaves knew they couldn't make it without Jesus' help. They wanted Jesus to guide their feet so that they would go in the right direction, hold their hands so they would not fall or stray from His path, and stand by them for reassurance and strength.

As we physically walk, it is necessary to move our feet and be directional in our steps. As we walk our Christian journey, we want the Lord to direct our spiritual steps and guide our lives. The Lord will help us as we walk on different terrains (trials, tribulations, and happiness), and He will hold our hand and guide us. Jesus is always with us. He never leaves or forsakes us.

The next time a situation arises that is too difficult to bear, know that your Heavenly Father is walking alongside of you. He will never leave you or forsake you. Trust Him as you walk with Him. Let Him lead and guide you.

Dear Lord, We thank you for your guidance as you walk with us. Thanks for your presence and for holding our hands as you guide us through life's journeys. Walk with us, Lord! Amen.

Songs Related to Walk:

1. I Want Jesus to Walk with Me - Negro Spiritual
2. Walking Up the King's Highway - Mary Gardner
                                            Thomas A. Dorsey
3. Walk Together Children - Negro Spiritual
4. Guide My Feet - Negro Spiritual

Walk (with me)

2 Corinthians 5:7

"We walk by faith, not by sight."

What is the result when we walk in our strength on our Christian journey? (Pause.) It is not advisable for Christians to walk in their own strength and on the knowledge they see with the naked eye. Guaranteed failure is a result for those who go it alone. John 15:5 states, "I am the vine, you are the branches. He who abides in Me, and I in him, bears much fruit; for without Me you can do nothing."

Our omniscient (all-knowing) God knows the plan of our lives. We need His guidance and direction. Have faith! Faith is believing what God says He will do. His promises are listed throughout the Bible. Therefore, walk and live by faith.

Although walking by faith may not be an easy walk, let the Lord direct each area of our lives and trust Him to lead us on the correct path. Each area of our lives includes financial decisions, relationships, marriages, rearing children, schooling, jobs, etc. However, when we see what is going on in and around us, we often may want to react, as we would want. We do not have the eyes of God. Open our eyes, Lord, as we walk by faith! Please lead and guide us.

Dear Lord, Just a closer walk with Thee makes it right. Walk with us, Lord. Help us, Lord, to keep our eyes on you and walk by faith and not by sight. We desire to walk in the right path with you leading and guiding our lives. Our prayer is to walk with you each and every day. When we stray, please lead us back to the correct path. Amen.

Songs Related to Walk:

1. Walk with Me Lord - Negro Spiritual

2. Just a Closer Walk with Thee - Unknown

3. I Want Jesus to Walk with Me - Negro Spiritual

4. Close to Thee - Fanny Crosby / Silas J. Vail

Seek

Matthew 6:33-34

"³³But seek ye first the kingdom of God, and his righteousness; and all these things shall be added unto you. ³⁴Take therefore no thought for the morrow: for the morrow shall take thought for the things of itself. Sufficient unto the day is the evil thereof."

The Lord knows what we need. Trust Him and His will for our lives. Don't go chasing rainbows, but chase after righteousness instead. Our righteousness lies in seeking God's ways and truths. Trust God's will for your life. When we seek after selfish pleasures and those things that do not please God or His plan for our lives, we invite trouble to enter. The unwanted trouble, bad situations, and turmoil that enter our lives when this occurs are completely unnecessary!

We want God's best for us. We want to live the Spirit-filled life that God has for us. Look to God for His direction and guidance. God has a plan for each of our lives. Seek His will and face. Spend time in His presence reading God's Word and in prayer. Let the Lord lead you every step of the way. He never ever leads us astray.

Dear Lord, Teach us how to seek you in all things. We want to honor you in all that we do. Help us to seek after your righteousness. Help us not to seek fame, riches, and land, but to seek after you. In Jesus' name, Amen.

Songs Related to Seek:

1. Seek Ye First - Karen Lafferty

2. The More I Seek You - Zach Neese

3. Let the Lord Lead You - Marlene Jenkins Cooper

4. Seek The Lord Who Is Now Present - Fred P. Green

Praise

Psalm 67:5

*"Let the people praise thee, God;
let all the people praise thee. What a joy it is to be able to
give God praise and let Him hear the praise from our lips!
He loves to hear the praises of His people for He inhabits
the praise of His people."*

There is so much to praise God for. What is the very first thing that comes to your mind when you think about what you can praise God for? (Pause.) We can praise Him for His excellent greatness, His works to the children of men, mighty acts, His son Jesus whom He sent to the earth to die and rise again for us, the new mercies we receive every morning, health, His faithfulness, His wisdom and guidance, for who He is, which is represented in His names, and many more.

A hymn writer wrote a song entitled, "O for a Thousand Tongues to Sing." If we had a thousand or even a million tongues, we could not praise God enough. David, the psalmist, loved to praise the Lord. David ends the Book of Psalms with six verses in Psalm 150. David states who should praise, where to praise, how to praise, when to praise, and what instruments we can use while praising God. Where? Praise Him anywhere. When? Praise Him at all times. How? Praise Him with instruments and with our lips. Who? Everyone who hath breath should praise the Lord. The word *praise* is mentioned in the Book of Psalms over 130 times. Praise God in the good times as well as in the bad times. Let all the people praise Thee!

Dear Lord, Please receive the praises from our lips today. We extol, honor, lift up your name and give you glory because you are worthy of our praise. The Word of God states in Psalm 150:6 that everything that hath breath praises the Lord. Praise ye the Lord. We aim to do that in our music and life. We offer our praise to you. Amen.

Songs Related to Praise:
1. Praise Jehovah - Beverly Crawford
2. Just Want To Praise You - Maurette Brown Clark
3. We Give You All The Praise - Alyn E. Waller
4. Hallelujah Praise the Lamb - Dawn Thomas
                              Gary McSpadden /Pam Thum

Sing

Psalm 149:1

"Praise ye the Lord. Sing unto the Lord a new song, and his praise in the congregation of saints."

We will sing of our Redeemer and all He has done for us. We will sing it from the rooftops, choir stand, pulpit, balcony, and in the congregation. Sing with thy whole heart. To sing is a verb; we need to actively do something. It is necessary for us to open our mouths, let the air from our lungs fill our diaphragms and flow between our vocal cords added with words from our lips. An even greater experience is when a group of people sings together in unison and harmony. The unified choir imparts a message unto the listener.

We have been given the joyous opportunity to lift our voices together in song in the worship service. We are choral messengers of song. Our choral pieces are not based on monosyllables, but we sing edifying words from the Bible and with text that is based on the Bible and Christian values. Let our personal lives match the words that we sing in our music message. Sing melodiously unto the God of our salvation.

Dear Lord, We offer up our praise to you through our voice. We lift you up, and we honor you today. You are worthy of our praise and the fruits of our lips. We pray you are blessed and pleased with our offering of praise. Let our words and melodies edify you, O Lord. Amen.

Songs Related to Sing:

1. Sing Unto The Lord A New Song -
                              Anthony (Tony) Wilkins
2. I'm Goin' a Sing When the Spirit Says Sing -
                    Negro Spiritual
3. With A Voice of Singing - Martin Shaw
4. Sing Hallelujah to the Lord - Linda Stassen

Risen

Matthew 28:5-6

"⁵And the angel answered and said unto the women, Fear not ye: for I know that ye seek Jesus, which was crucified. ⁶He is not here: for he is risen, as he said. Come, see the place where the Lord lay."

Can you imagine the scene as Mary Magdalene, Mary the mother of James, and Salome arrived at the tomb and Jesus was not there? (Mark 16:1) Imagine their amazement. They witnessed the death and burial of Jesus. Where is He? The angel said, "… He is not here." (Mark 16:6) Then the angel gave them an assignment to go tell the disciples that Jesus is not here in the tomb; He has risen from the grave. Yes, they delivered the great news. (Most women love to share great news.)

The fact that He is risen is great news. Jesus has broken the curse and penalty of sin and death by rising up from the grave. He left His burial clothes right there in the tomb. We are not bound by sin and death. Jesus paid the price for us on Calvary. We are free! Because Christ arose from the grave, we can have eternal life if we accept this free gift of salvation.

Dear Lord, You are risen, indeed. Up from the grave, you arose. You conquered death and the grave. We are so grateful. Thank you, Jesus for praying the price of our salvation. Amen.

Songs Related to Risen:

1. Christ The Lord Is Risen Today - Charles Wesley
2. Up From The Grave He Arose - Robert Lowry
3. Because He Lives - Gloria & William Gaither
4. In Christ Alone - Keith Getty / Stuart Townsend

Knees

Ephesians 3:14

"For this cause I bow my knees unto the Father of our Lord Jesus Christ."

What a blessing to be able to get on our knees and pray to our Lord and Savior Jesus Christ! However, we only need arthritis, surgery, or one sport injury that involves our knees, thighs, or ankle to keep us from praying on our knees. Bowing down on our knees is an act of humble submission unto the Lord. "When I fall on my knees," wrote the slaves in the Negro Spiritual entitled "Let Us Break Bread Together." It is understandable that some people cannot bow down on their knees.

"And it was so, that when Solomon had made an end of praying all this prayer and supplication unto the Lord, he arose from before the altar of the Lord, from kneeling on his knees with his hands spread up to heaven." (I Kings 8:54) What a beautiful picture of Solomon praying to the Lord.

Our heavenly Father knows our hearts and hears our

prayers, whether we are literally on our knees or not. Pray! Our Father wants to hear from us.

Dear Lord, We bow in humble submission as we lift our hearts to you today. Whether we are physically on our knees or not, we give you glory and honor. Please bless the hearers of this devotional, rehearsal, service, and time of prayer. Amen.

Songs Related to Knees:

1. I Bowed On My Knees and Cried Holy -
   Nuttie Dudley Washington / E.M. Dudley Cantwell
2. Let Us Break Bread Together - Negro Spiritual
3. Fall On My Knees - Matthew Browder
4. Every Knee Shall Bow - Twila Paris

Clouds

1 Thessalonians 4:16-17

"¹⁶For the Lord himself shall descend from heaven with a shout, with the voice of the archangel, and with the trump of God: and the dead in Christ shall rise first: ¹⁷Then we which are alive and remain shall be caught up together with them in the clouds, to meet the Lord in the air: and so shall we ever be with the Lord."

The sky and its clouds are located above the earth. Lift up your heads and see the sky. Colors of the sky vary in many hues, while clouds are usually white or black. According to the National Weather Service, there are ten basic types of clouds.

Nonetheless, when Jesus returns back to the earth, we won't be identifying the clouds as He breaks through the sky, but looking unto Jesus who will come for those who have accepted Him as their personal Savior, and for those who are dead and asleep in Christ. (1 Thessalonians 4:14) We are waiting for His appearance and return. Or imagine hearing the trumpet sound when you are at the grocery store. No matter where we may be when He returns, we want to see Jesus and go with Him to heaven, to that place that is prepared for us. The author and finisher of our faith is Jesus!

Dear Lord, As you ascended in the heavens over 2,000 years ago, you promised that you will return. We wait upon your return, dear Father. Until that day, we pray that our music and testimonies reach others for the Kingdom, and bless and honor your Holy Name through our musical offering to you. Amen.

Songs Related to Clouds:

1. We Shall Behold Him - Dottie Rambo
2. Days of Elijah - Robin Mark
3. I'll Be Caught Up To Meet Him -

James Cleveland

4. The Uncloudy Day - Josiah Kelley Alwood

Lamb of God

John 1:29

"The next day John seeth Jesus coming unto him, and saith, Behold the Lamb of God, which taketh away the sin of the world."

Our scripture today was spoken by John the Baptist. He was the son of Zacharias and Elizabeth, who was related to Mary, the mother of Jesus. (Luke 1) John the Baptist was given the assignment to prepare the way of the Lord before Jesus started His ministry. John did what was asked of him, to announce the coming of Jesus and to baptize him.

John the Baptist was a messenger and completed his assignment. He preached about the coming kingdom and the need for people to repent of their sins. We are messengers of Christ too. Our assignment is to witness to the lost and dying by telling them about Jesus Christ, His saving grace, and how they can have eternal life. (Mark 16:15)

When John saw Jesus, he said, "Behold the Lamb of God, which taketh away the sin of the world." Jesus Christ sacrificed His life on Calvary as a sacrificial lamb. He is the Lamb of God.

Dear Lord, O Lamb of God, who sacrificed Your life for us. We thank you for sacrificing your life for us by dying on the cross for our sins. We exalt and honor you today. Where would we be if this act of selflessness were not done for us? We give you glory, O Lamb of God. Amen.

Songs Related to Lamb of God:

1. Lamb of God - Twila Paris
2. Worthy is the Lamb - Don Wyrtzen
3. Now Behold the Lamb - Kirk Franklin
4. Hallelujah Praise the Lamb (chorus) - Dawn Thomas
                                    Gary McSpadden / Pam Thum

Hills

1 Kings 20:28

"And there came a man of God, and spake unto the king of Israel, and said, 'Thus saith the Lord, Because the Syrians have said, The Lord is God of the hills, but he is not God of the valleys, therefore will I deliver all this great multitude into thine hand, and ye shall know that I am the Lord."

Some people incorporate climbing hills while on a walking regime. Others change the dials on the treadmill to adjust the platform to a particular level or degree of incline. Extra energy is required when running or walking on an incline. It is phenomenal to experience our pedometers (i.e., Fitbit, Garmin, Apple watches) automatically noting when our feet have encountered an incline. Runners and walkers look for a varied and rich exercise workout.

Our Lord was not looking for exhilarating exercise while climbing Hill of Calvary with a cross on His back. It was cruel of the Roman soldiers to have Him carry His cross to the top of the hill. He had to use much energy to walk up the hill, carrying the cross on which he would be crucified.

There are eight verses in the King James version of the Bible that have the words *hills* and *valleys* in the same verse. In the verse from 1 Kings 20, the Syrians didn't believe God was the God of hills and valleys. We will walk up hills and go down in the valleys, but be of good cheer. Although a hill is upwards and a valley is downwards, God gives us the strength we need for the journey. Our God is the God of hills and valleys. While in the valley, look to the hills, from whence cometh our help; for our help cometh from the Lord, who made heaven and earth. (Psalm 121:1-2) Rely on God's strength!

Dear Lord, Walk with us! While on this tedious journey, please guide our feet while we climb the hills and mountains and as we walk in and around the valleys. Amen.

Songs Related to Hills:
1. On A Hill Called Calvary - Patricia & Ronald Owens
2. Climbing Up the Mountain - Negro Spiritual
3. I Believe in a Hill Called Mount Calvary - Dale Oldham
Gloria Gaither / William J. Gaither
4. He Owns The Cattle On A Thousand Hills -
John W. Peterson

Pastures

Psalm 23:2

"He maketh me to lie down in green pastures: he leadeth me beside the still waters."

No matter if you reside in a metropolitan city, in the country, or suburbia, most places have parks filled with trees, grass, flowers, and maybe a body of water. Two of the largest metropolitan parks in the United States are Central Park in New York City and Fairmount Park in Philadelphia, Pennsylvania. Although these parks are in a city environment, one can possibly get the same feel of the green pastures "vibe" that David experienced while sitting amongst the waters and luscious green grass in ancient pastoral times. Sitting by the brook, lying on the grass in a shaded area can bring about a calmness that soothes the soul.

When we were babies and toddlers, many of us were made to lie down and take a nap. Some of us had to take a nap because we were restless and others because they were on a fixed naptime schedule. When we awoke, our bodies were rested and we were raring to go. As young adults and older adults, we need to remember to be still, rest, and lie down, and let Jesus speak to us. Jesus gives calmness and speaks to our souls. Relax and listen to the voice of the Lord. He leads us!

Dear Lord, Please lead us. Lead us as we lay still in pastures green. Speak to us as the waters roll in the stream in beautiful harmony and rippling rhythms. Calm our souls when we are weary and stressed. Help us to rely on you, dear Father. Amen.

Songs Related to Pastures:

1. Savior Like a Shepherd Lead Us - Dorothy Ann Thrupp

William Batchelder Bradbury

2. The New 23rd - Ralph Carmichael

3. The Lord's My Shepherd - Francis Rous Jessie

Seymour Irvine / William Whittingham

4. God Leads Us Along - George A. Young

Blessings

Ephesians 1:3

"Blessed be the God and Father of our Lord Jesus Christ, who hath blessed us with all spiritual blessings in heavenly places in Christ."

When we think of the blessings that we have received, what is the first thing that comes to your mind? (Pause.) There are no wrong answers. One might say their salvation; another may say their great measure of health. Financial blessings through their occupation may be the blessings of some people.

Now let us think of spiritual blessings. What comes to mind? (Pause.) Spiritual blessings are the benefits we receive as Christians. Some of those spiritual blessings are our inheritance, which is in heaven, eternal life, and our redemption through the blood of Jesus, to name a few. Let's not just sing of His blessings, but also bless the Lord with our words in prayer, adoration, and exaltation. We give thanks to God for all the spiritual blessings that He has bestowed upon us.

Dear Lord, We are so grateful for all the spiritual blessings that we have received and the ones on their way. No other can give spiritual blessings but you, and for that we are grateful. We are humbled by the gift of your spiritual blessings. We give thanks to thee. Amen.

Songs Related to Blessing:

1. Come, Thou Fount of Every Blessing -
                    Robert Robinson / John Wyeth
2. Bless His Holy Name (Bless The Lord) -
                    Andrae Crouch
3. Praise God from Whom All Blessings Flow -   Isaac Watts / William Keathe / John Hatton
4. There Shall Be Showers of Blessings –
        Daniel Webster Whittle / James McGranahan

Hallelujah

Revelation 19:1

"And after these things I heard a great voice of much people in heaven, saying, Alleluia; Salvation, and glory, and honour, and power, unto the Lord our God."

"Hallelu, Hallelu, Hallelujah Praise Ye the Lord" is the title of a popular children's song. Children sing this fun and exuberant song in Vacation Bible School, Sunday School, children's bible study, and Christian day and overnight camps. Children repeat the words *hallelu, hallelujah, praise,* and *ye the Lord* multiple times throughout the song.

This song is also considered an action song. Children stand and sit during specific passages. The words are sung with exuberance, with glee on their faces. The children who sing this song are taught and learn early in life how to praise the Lord.

Because of the message, melody, and song familiarity, the author of this devotional has used this children's song during Sunday morning's praise and worship time at church. As adults and young people, we should never forget why and how to praise the Lord. "Hallelu, Hallelu, Hallelujah Praise Ye the Lord" is a song that keeps that remembrance alive in our minds. The Lord is so worthy to be praised.

Dear Lord, We give you praise today, our dear Father. Our words of hallelujah offer praises unto you. We praise you for who you are and for your wondrous works. Lord, we thank you and praise you this day. Amen.

Songs Related to Hallelujah:

1. Hallelujah - Traditional
2. Hallelujah Chorus - George Frideric Handel
3. Hallelujah - Mark Condon
4. Alleluia (Agnus Dei) - Michael Smith

Glory

John 12:28

"Father, glorify thy name. Then came there a voice from heaven, saying, I have both glorified it, and will glorify it again."

The Greek word for *glory* is "doxa." A simple definition for glory is to honor and give praise. All glory belongs to God. We glorify the Lord in our worship, adoration, in our reverence of Him, through our songs, and all that we do. No one should receive glory but God. We recognize who God is through His glory. We glorify His name, works, and attributes. When people sing or talk about God's glory filling a given space, such as the temple or the sanctuary, this can be an unexplainable experience. "Oh, the Glory of Your Presence" is one song that seeks to explain the presence of the Lord through music.

As church musicians and singers, it is our ministry, duty, and obligation to sing and play songs that glorify God and Him only. God is worthy of our praise and adoration. Let's give God the glory that is due Him. Edwin Hawkins, the famed gospel composer, in his song, "Give Glory to God," reminds the listener of the importance of giving God the glory. The verses talk about lifting and raising our hands in recognition of His glory. Hallelujah, give glory to God!

Dear God, Glory and honor are yours today and every day. You alone are worthy. We lift our voices and play our instruments in praise to you. Amen.

Songs Related to Glory:

1. Oh the Glory of Your Presence - Steven L. Fry

2. Give Glory To God - Edwin Hawkins

3. With A Voice of Singing - Martin Shaw

4. Glorify Thy Name - Gloria Adkins

Glory and Honor

1 Peter 1:7

"That the trial of your faith, being much more precious than of gold that perisheth, though it be tried with fire, might be found unto praise and honour and glory at the appearing of Jesus Christ."

Glory, honor, and *praise* are three words often linked together in Christian worship, song, and conversation. These words should only be linked to one person, God. He alone deserves the glory, honor, and praise. There is none other.

How do we give God glory? We give Him glory by acknowledging the fact of who God is, and that there is none other. We offer praise to Him with the words of our mouth, by lifting our hands toward heaven, clapping our hands, and dancing (if you wish) in His presence.

The trials of our faith should give God glory. How? People watch our lives and how we experience life. Most of our lives have not been on a *"bed of roses."* When a trial is over, giving God glory for His keeping power should be on our lips and hearts. God has done marvelous things in our life, for which we should be glad. Our lives and all that we do should glorify God. Give glory to God! "O sing unto the Lord a new song; for he hath done marvellous things: his right hand, and his holy arm, hath gotten him the victory." (Psalm 98:1)

Dear Lord, We pray that in all we do, Lord, you get the glory. For you alone are worthy of all glory, honor, and praise. We acknowledge who you are. In Jesus' name, Amen.

Songs Related to Glory:

1. Give Him the Glory - Clint Brown / Mattie Moss Clark
2. My Tribute (To God be the Glory) - Andrae Crouch
3. Glory to His Name - Elisha Albright Hoffman
                              John Hart Stockton
4. To God be the Glory - Fanny Jane Crosby
                              William Howard Doane

Look

Titus 2:13

"Looking for that blessed hope, and the glorious appearing of the great God and our Savior Jesus Christ;"

As Christians, our hope is in Jesus Christ. Our Savior will return to the earth to rapture His believers in Christ. People all over the globe who don't believe in Jesus do not have this hope. Their hope is in other people and things such as alcohol, food, drugs, and sex. Without the hope of our Savior, people try to fill the void. However, other people and earthly things will fail us in that effort, but Jesus never fails. People are seeking and looking for what is missing in their lives, and we pray that if they hear our music, they will hear the message of our hope, which is in Christ Jesus.

We are blessed to have a hope, which is rooted and based in Jesus Christ. When situations in our lives look hopeless, we are to look to Jesus, our blessed hope. We have hope! Let's lift our voices and sing beautiful music that rings out for all to hear and know that Jesus Christ is coming back for His children. Jesus Christ, our blessed hope.

Dear Lord, One day soon, the sky will crack open and you will appear. We know that day is swiftly approaching. The signs of the times are solidifying your return. We shall behold you. Even so, come Lord Jesus. Amen.

Songs Related to Look:

1. We Shall Behold Him - Dottie Rambo

2. My Faith Looks Up to Thee - Ray Palmer

3. Looking Unto Jesus - Mac Lynch

4. Look and Live (I've a Message From the Lord) -

William Augustine Ogden

Clouds

Revelation 1:7

"Behold, he cometh with clouds; and every eye shall see him, and they also which pierced him: and all kindreds of the earth shall wail because of him. Even so, Amen."

Can you remember your sixth-grade science lesson on clouds? Who remembers what clouds are made of and the names of the clouds? To revive your memory, a cloud is made up of water and ice crystals found in the air. Cumuliform, Stratus, Cumulus, Stratocumulus, Altostratus are five of the ten types of clouds, all of which have Latin names.

According to the atmosphere, different clouds form in the sky each and every day in every part of the world. Scientists can determine which clouds will form based on their scientific instruments and knowledge of the elements. However, we don't know what type of clouds Jesus will appear through nor when He will crack the sky and come for His children. (Do you ever wonder what key the trumpet will sound in?) Our scripture reference tells us that Jesus will break through the clouds. The Second Coming of

Christ is quickly approaching. We will soon look up and see Him breaking through the clouds. He is coming! Keep looking for His return. Look up! Even so, come Lord Jesus.

Dear Lord, There are so many terrible things happening in our world today. We believe the signs of the times are present and that your return is very soon. Even so, come Lord Jesus. Amen.

Songs Related to Clouds:
1. We Shall Behold Him - Dottie Rambo
2. Revelation 19:1 - A. Jeffrey LaValley
3. Days Of Elijah - Robin Mark
4. Lo! He Comes With Clouds Descending -

Charles Wesley

And They Sang (Singing as I Go)

2 Chronicles 29:30

"Moreover Hezekiah the king and the princes commanded the Levites to sing praises unto the Lord with the words of David, and of Asaph the seer. And they sang praises with gladness, and they bowed their heads and worshipped."

Who sings hymns and spiritual songs when in trouble? Paul and Silas sang while in a Roman jail. Paul told the believers in Ephesus "to sing and make music in your heart to the Lord" (Ephesians 5:19). Paul took his own advice, and look what happened! The doors of the jail opened while he was singing and praising the Lord in song.

The disciples sang a hymn after the Last Supper with Jesus and on their way to the Mount of Olives (Matthew 26:30). The Bible does not give us the titles of the songs they were singing. In many churches, the congregation sings "The Blood Will Never Lose Its Power" by Andrae Crouch, "Jesus Keep Me Near the Cross" by Fanny Crosby. Some churches, during the ordinance of communion, sing the old Negro Spiritual "Remember Me," which repeats the words "remember me" multiple times.

38

Thomas Dorsey decided to compose the song "Precious Lord" when his wife and son died during childbirth. The author of *Grace Notes* wrote seven songs while in the midst of a terrible life event. Many composers write in times of overwhelming tragedy and sadness. Take the Apostle Paul's advice and sing and make music in your heart to the Lord. Singing doesn't take all the pain away, but it can soothe the heartache. And they sang . . .

Dear Heavenly Father, there is a song in our hearts, one of praise, worship, and adoration. It's our desire to sing with a loud voice and softly when appropriate. We want to use our voice to lift up your name and give you glory. Also let the words of our hymns, spiritual songs, choruses, and praise and worship music heal and soothe our souls and the listeners in Jesus' name. When we cannot find a song of praise to sing, please place one in our hearts. Amen.

Songs Related to And They Sang:
1. He Keeps Me Singing - Luther B. Bridgers
2. With A Voice of Singing - Martin Shaw
3. Come, Christians, Join And Sing –

Christian H. Bateman
4. I'm Going To Keep On Singing - Andrae Crouch

Hands

Lamentations 3:41

"Let us lift up our heart with our hands unto God
in the heavens."

Our hands can do many things. We can lift them to the Lord in praise, bring them together to pray in humble submission, and clap while rejoicing in song. Our hands can play instruments, give a touch, create beautiful works of art, give motion and direction, and conduct beautiful music. But our hands can do evil as well. They can hit, slap, steal, kill, and destroy. Jesus used His hands to give sight to the blind, heal many diseases, throw the moneychangers out of the synagogue, perform miracles, and make things as a carpenter. He used his hands to do good.

Our hands are an extension of our body, and they operate based on what we tell them to do. Like Jesus, let us use our hands to do good. Let's lift our hands in praise, and, like the Psalmist, "Clap your hands, all ye people."

Dear Lord, We praise you today because of who you are. We praise you for you mighty acts! We clap our hands in praise of you today. We lift our hands in humble adoration. There is none like you. We lift our hands and offer up our praise. Amen.

Songs Related to Hands:

1. We Lift Our Hands in the Sanctuary - Kurt Carr

2. I Know the Lord's Laid His Hands on Me -

Negro Spiritual

3. He's Got the Whole World in His Hands –

Negro Spiritual

4. Lift Up Your Hands To The Lord - Fred Hammond

Mildred Hammond / Noel Hall

Salt

Matthew 5:13

"Ye are the salt of the earth: but if the salt have lost his savour, wherewith shall it be salted? it is thenceforth good for nothing, but to be cast out, and to be trodden under foot of men."

Who remembers the scientific name and chemical formula for salt? (Pause.) If you said sodium chloride or NaCl, you are right. Salt has many purposes, one of which is to add flavor. Cooks often salt their dishes to bring out the flavor. As Christians, the Lord commands us in Matthew 5 to salt the earth.

Do the words of our songs and music salt the earth? The Bible says we are the salt of the earth. Does our music, lives, Christian walk, and spoken words bring salt to the earth? Salt changes the taste of food. Most foods lack salt and need just a pinch or more to make it better. Our goal as Christians is to be the salt of the earth. Let's flavor our earth with our kind words, lives that reflect Christ, the message of Christ, and Christian songs.

Dear Lord, We see and hear the command in Matthew 5, to salt the earth. We ask for strength, power, and the willingness to do just that. Help us to have the spirit to live holy and speak truth. Hear our prayer, O Lord. Amen.

Songs Related to Salt:

1. Say So - Israel Houghton / Michael Gungor

2. Salt and Light - Jan & John L'Ecuyer

3. We are the Salt and Light - Larry Holder

4. We are the Salt of the Earth - Gary Lanier

Cast

1 Peter 5:7

"Cast all your cares on Him."

Are you loaded down with heavy burdens? Are life's travails getting you down and making you sad? The Bible has the solution for each one of us. It's not a pill, mantra, exercise, or regiment. The Bible simply tells us to cast all of our cares on Him. This may seem too easy, but it is difficult for some of us to lay down our burdens at the feet of Jesus. We want to be in control. And how is that working out for you? Lean on the everlasting arms of Jesus. He will carry us through.

It's a blessing that children are taught the "Cares Chorus" in church, Christian camps, and Vacation Bible School. Children are taught at an early age to give their cares to Jesus. As adults, we should never forget to take our burdens to the Lord and leave them at His feet.

What burdens and problems are you holding onto today? Release them. In Matthew 11:30, the Lord said, "For my yoke is easy and my burden is light." Negro slaves sang the song "Down By The Riverside," which talked about laying down their burdens down by the riverside. Give those burdens to the Lord. Now! Do not wait. Who wants to carry a heavy load? If someone else wants to carry it, here it is. Jesus explicitly said to give Him our burdens. Praise the Lord. Lift and unload the burdens. Lay your burdens at the cross. Lay them at the feet of Jesus.

Dear Lord, We humbly lift our voices to you today. We know we are supposed to cast all of our cares on you. We sometimes forget to do so. Because of our circumstances, we sometimes forget to lay our burdens down at your feet. We know that you can handle each of our circumstances and situations. We lay our burdens at your feet. It's yours, Lord. Thank you. Amen.

Songs Related to Cast:

1. Cares Chorus - Kelly Willard
2. Hiya Hiya (Cast Your Burdens on Jesus) -

                                        Isaac G. W. Balinda
3. Cast Thy Burden Upon The Lord - Felix Mendelssohn
4. Learning to Lean - John Stallings

Power

Romans 1:16

"For I am not ashamed of the gospel of Christ:
for it is the power of God unto salvation to
every one that believeth; to the Jew first,
and also to the Greek."

When Jesus was crucified, buried, and rose again on the third day, He had all power in His hand to complete each of these tasks. No superheroes—Superman, Batman, Superwomen, Flash, Captain America, Spiderman or The Black Panther from Wakanda—had the power that Jesus has. No one else can do this, has done this, or will do we tapped into the power of the Almighty God this. Jesus has the power!

When Jesus' blood was shed for us on Calvary, His omniscient power paid the price for sin, and He rose on the third day. Tap into the source—the source is Jesus. How do we tap into the source? By reading, believing, and studying The Bible and praying. Jesus has the power. Tap into Jesus' power.

Dear Lord, God the Father in heaven and earth gives all power unto you. No one can compare to you. Others have tried and have not succeeded. We have even constructed fake superheroes, but they all lack the power of God. We rely on your power and strength. It gives us great joy to sing about the mighty power of God. Amen.

Songs Related to Power:

1. There Is Power In The Blood -

Lewis Edgar Jones

2. I Sing the Mighty Power of God - Isaac Watts

Xavier Ludwig Hartig

3. Break Every Chain - Will Reagan

4. All Hail The Power of Jesus' Name -

Edward Perronet (Text)

Presence

Psalm 16:11

Thou wilt shew me the path of life: in thy presence is
fulness of joy; at thy right hand there are
pleasures for evermore."

If we receive the fullness of joy in His presence, who wouldn't want to be in His presence? What a pleasure and honor to be in the presence of the Lord! Have you ever been in the presence of a great man or woman, and you felt so elated with the experience? Imagine how much greater of an experience you can have with the Lord as you come together with other believers to worship and pray to Him. What an awesome privilege and opportunity to commune with Him and be in His presence! David was so elated about this fact that he wrote about his experience in the Book of Psalms. In Psalm 84:2, David states that he longed to be in the courts of the Lord. He further describes being in the presence of the Lord in Psalm 91.

According to today's scripture, David explains in detail what happens when we are in the presence of the Lord. If we get into a relationship with the Lord by praying, reading His Word, and spending time with Him, we will reap so many benefits. Come let us worship the Lord. Come into His Presence!

Dear Lord, As we come before you in your presence, we humble ourselves, lift up holy hands, bless, and praise your holy name. There is none like you. We magnify you, extol you, and thank you for all you do in our lives. There is none like you. We bless you! Amen and Amen.

Songs Related to Presence:

1. Surely The Presence Of The Lord - Lanny Wolfe

2. Holy Ground - Geron Davis

3. Oh The Glory of His Presence - Steve Fry

4. O Thou in Whose Presence - Joseph Swain

Late

John 11:21

"Then said Martha unto Jesus, Lord, if thou hadst been here, my brother had not died."

It is amazing how people in our congregations have different views on the element of time. Some parishioners arrive an hour before the start of worship service, others fifteen minutes prior to start time, others right at the appointed time, and some miss the mark and arrive late.

Some people believe that to be early is to arrive five to fifteen minutes ahead of the designated time. We do not have to worry about God's timeliness. God is always on time. Time doesn't define God.

Some thought Jesus was late when he showed up after Lazarus died. This notion of being late was applied by His friends, disciples, and our standards. Lazarus died. "If only," said Martha. Jesus was not late. We sometime say crazy things when our circumstances look bleak, hopeless, or beyond our understanding. Jesus doesn't operate in any of the time zones in our world. When waiting for God to move, fix, or settle circumstances in our lives, trust God's schedule. He's never late.

Dear Lord, God you are an on-time God. You are never late! You don't even operate in our time zones. We can depend on God. You will be there on time. Thanks for readiness. We are waiting on you. Amen.

Songs Related to Late:
1. He's An On Time God - Dottie Peoples
2. In His Time - Diane Ball
3. In Time On Time Every Time - Belinda Lee Smith
4. Take Time To Be Holy - George Coles Stebbins
                                    William Dunn Longstaff

Joy

Galatians 5:23-24

"But the fruit of the Spirit is love, joy, peace, longsuffering, gentleness, goodness, faith, meekness, temperance: against such there is no law."

Joy is the second of the nine fruits of the spirit. We want the joy that comes because we believe in Jesus and are filled with the Spirit, not just happiness. Happiness and joy are two different experiences. Happiness is an experience that happens because of an event. But joy is an emotion that resonates in our heart.

It is Jesus' desire that we experience joy. Joy cannot be found in a bottle of Barbados rum, nor in great amounts of money in our pockets or bank account. Knowing Jesus and having a relationship with Him gives us joy. When sadness does come due to bad situations, circumstances or trials, the Bible states that joy comes in the morning. (Psalm 30:5)

When you're sad, sing joyful songs. Singing makes the heart glad. We must take the focus off of ourselves and our sadness. Ephesians 5:19 states, "Speaking to yourselves in psalms and hymns and spiritual songs, singing and making melody in your heart to the Lord..." What songs lift your spirits? Pause and think about them. We shall not forget! Sing with joy! Sing with the joy that resonates deep in your heart.

Dear Lord, Joy! True joy only comes from knowing you. We thank thee for the unspeakable joy that only you can give. May others hear and see the joy in our hearts, music, and lives. Amen.

Songs Related to Joy:

1. Joyful Joyful We Adore Thee - Henry Van Dyke
Ludwig Beethoven
2. Joy To The World - George F. Handel / Isaac Watts
3. Joy Joy - Edwin Hawkins
4. The Joy of the Lord is My Strength - Alliene Vale

Angels

Luke 2:10

"And the angel said unto them, Fear not: for, behold,
I bring you good tidings of great joy,
which shall be to all people."

In the Bible, there are many references to the words spoken by, appearances of, and actions performed by the angels. Angels are messengers of the Lord. For example, "The angel of the Lord said unto her" (Genesis 16:9-11), "the angel of the Lord appeared unto him" (Judges 6:12), "the angel that talked with me said unto me" (Zechariah 1:9), "And the angel answered and said unto the women" (Matthew 28:5), "And the angel said unto her" (Luke 1:30), and "the angel of the Lord by night opened the prison doors" (Acts 5:19).

At specific times, God uses angels to speak for Him. Gabriel and Michael's names are identified as angels, whereas just the word *angel* identifies others in the Bible. Angels played instruments. They are no strangers to music. Gabriel played his trumpet. In modern times, people often state that the choir sounds like angels. As musicians and artists, we sing, play, and dance God's message from the Word of God.

Dear Lord, May our message in song be pleasing to you. May the melodies, harmonies, rhythms, and words sound just as the angels would sound. All of our praises are for you. Amen.

Songs Related to Angels:
1. Ten Thousand Angels - Ray Overholt
2. Angels We Have Heard on High –
            Edward Shippen Barnes / James Chadwick
3. Angels From the Realms of Glory -
            Henry Thomas Smart / James Montgomery
4. All Night All Day - Negro Spiritual

Faithfulness

1 Corinthians 1:9

"God is faithful, by whom ye were called unto the fellowship of his Son Jesus Christ our Lord."

Forgetfulness! Is it possible to forget that our God is always faithful to His children? Forgetfulness is not in God's vocabulary. Take a moment and note three acts of His faithfulness to you in the last week. Our God is faithful. He is dependable, trustworthy, and always present. He is for us!

Sometimes, we are not faithful to him. Sometimes we are not faithful, dependable, or we are just slothful in our ministry to Him or what He has called us to do. How would you rate your faithfulness to God? Can God depend on you?

Sometimes the accuser, the devil, may speak words of discouragement to you. When this happens, speak the Word of God to yourself and out loud. 1 Thessalonians 5:24 states, "Faithful is he that calleth you, who also will do it."

He has called you to be faithful. Let us do our best for the Master. God has been faithful to us in every way.

Dear Lord, You are faithful. You are dependable. We stand on your Word. Thanks for your faithfulness to us. Amen.

Songs Related to Faithfulness:
1. Faithful is Our God - Hezekiah Walker
2. Great is Thy Faithfulness - Thomas O. Chisholm
   William Marion Runyan
3. Lord, You've Been Faithful - Ron Hamilton
   Cheryl Reid
4. We Can Depend On God - Charles H. Nicks Jr.

Care

Mark 4:38

"And he was in the hinder part of the ship, asleep on a pillow: and they awake him, and say unto him, Master, carest thou not that we perish?"

No job? Sick in the hospital? Finances challenged? Sadness in your life? Have you ever spoken the words "No one cares for me" or "I am here all by myself"? Sometimes we have a solo pity party all by ourselves.

Does Jesus care? The disciples asked the very same question. Jesus and the disciples were out to sea in a boat. All of a sudden, the sea became turbulent, with high winds and waves. Jesus was asleep during this time, but the disciples were awake and scared. They woke Him up and asked, "Master, carest thou not that we perish?" (Mark 4:38c) Jesus woke up, rebuked the wind, and said to the sea, "Peace Be Still." (Mark 4:39) The sea relaxed. Jesus said to the disciples, "Why are ye so fearful? how is it that ye have no faith?" (Mark 4:40)

Yes, He cares for you and me! He is our protector and shepherd. He cares for His sheep. Our shepherd cares about each aspect of our lives. Know that we are on His radar. Saints of God, "Why are ye so fearful? how is it that ye have no faith?" Do you fear that God does not care for you? Caring for us is on His list. God cares for each of us!

Dear Lord, Casting our care on you lifts our burdens. Our heavy burdens become light because you take them from us. Does Jesus care for me? Yes, Lord. Thank you, Amen.

Songs Related to Care:

1. Does Jesus Care? - Frank E. Graeff / Joseph L Hall
2. God Cares - Rosie Wallace
3. Cares Chorus - Kelly Willard
4. God Will Take Care of You - Civilla Durfee Martin
Walter Stillman Martin

Miracle

John 12:37

"But though he had done so many miracles before them,
yet they believed not on him:"

After watching Jesus perform miracles, how is it that the scribes, Sadducees, and others still didn't believe? Why did they not believe? They were blind; their hearts were hard. In John 12:4, John states that "He hath blinded their eyes, and hardened their heart; that they should not see with their eyes, nor understand with their heart, and be converted, and I should heal them."

In the New Testament, Jesus performed over thirty-five miracles. Jesus still performs miracles today. People are not walking on water like Peter did with Jesus in the New Testament. However, today Jesus heals, delivers, and sets the captive free. Have you heard of a computing glitch that wiped debts out and placed an account as paid-in-full? Have you heard a doctor say that the disease is no longer present? Sometimes Jesus performs miracles without others praying for us. We can pray for ourselves! Sometimes Jesus empowers others to pray and aid in our miracles. Jehovah

Rapha, my healer; Jehovah Jireh, my provider. God is still in the miracle business. Miracles are happening today. We believe!

Dear Jesus, The miracle worker. We enter into your presence today with humble hearts; we acknowledge that you are the Lord of miracles. We pray for those here in this room that need a miracle from you. We're asking you for healing powers in all situations. In Jesus' name, Amen.

Songs Related to Miracle:

1. It's A Miracle - Gloria Gaither / William Gaither
2. I'm Looking For A Miracle - Clark Sisters
3. It Took a Miracle - John W. Peterson
4. Waitin' On A Miracle - Matthew West

Tribulation

John 16:33

"These things I have spoken unto you, that in me ye might have peace. In the world ye shall have tribulation: but be of good cheer; I have overcome the world."

Tests, trials, and tribulations are not always a result of sin. Many difficulties come to strengthen our faith. When we are faced with hard times, how do we go through the journey? What verses do you hold on to, repeat, post on your wall, and speak out loud? What confessions come out of our mouths?

Today's verse states that we will have tribulations. Some will have more than others, but there is no escaping them. Don't seek out troubles and tribulations, but be ready and prepared when they occur. James states, "Consider it pure joy, my brothers, whenever you face trials of many kinds" (James 1:2). Victory! Jesus has overcome the world.

Dear Lord, Today we are careful and mindful that tribulations will come our way. With your help, we will hold onto the Word of God for strength, comfort, and power. Help us, Lord! Please help the congregation or our audiences accept our words of encouragement through our songs. May we be encouraged as well. Amen.

Songs Related to Tribulation:
1. T Is For Trials and Tribulations - Stuart Ross
2. Our Help Is In The Name of the Lord - David Baroni
3. Mighty Long Way - Joe Pace II
4. The Only Hope We Have - Margaret Aikens-Jenkins

Praise

John 12:43

"For they loved the praise of men more than the praise of God."

Who is John speaking of in today's scripture verse? He couldn't possibly be talking about me or my choir partner, or the soprano section. Becoming prideful after ministering in song is not God's way. Prideful singing is not ministering to the body of Christ.

What is prideful singing? Here are a few examples. "I did that." "I know the people were blessed with my solo." "Our choir sings that song better than that choir." "Look at me! I know you will be blessed with my voice today." These silent or vocalized statements do not focus on God, but on people. Prideful singing can be outwardly seen, as well as wholly hidden, though it is still there. We should check ourselves and reflect on our attitude of music ministry. Do not let the praises of people take away from God's glory. Beware! Many people love the praise of men, but we need to keep such praise in perspective. Accept the adulation with graciousness, but send that praise right back to God. There is a thin line where we can cross over and take God's praises. Satan does not want glory, honor, and attention going to God either. God is not his friend. Every praise belongs to God and God alone.

We sing, dance, and play our instruments for Jesus' glory and His praise only. But what happens if pride creeps into our spirit? We confess it to God and do better next time. Prideful singing can be a personal thing or done as a group. No one should get God's glory, but Him! Give Him the glory and give Him the praise. He alone is worthy. Let's give God the praise. Praise is what we do. Hallelujah!

Dear Lord, May the words of our ministry in song from our lips and the melodies that we play with our hands bring you joy. Let our praise for thee be acceptable in your sight. All praises to you. Amen.

Songs Related to Praise:
1. Praise Him Praise Him – Chester Allen / Fanny Crosby
2. Every Praise - Hezekiah Walker / John Bratton
3. Praise The Name of Jesus - Roy Hicks Jr.
4. Doxology - Thomas Ken / Tommy Walker

All

1 Chronicles 29:14b
"All things come of thee, and of thine own
have we given thee."

Many composers have set the above offertory text to music. The well-known Classical-Romantic composer Ludwig Beethoven was one of the first composers to set the text to music. His tune is sung in many churches as an offertory response. There are over seventy-five hymnals that carry this song in their hymnal.

We return a portion of what God has allowed us to receive back to Him through our place of worship. Nonetheless, all that we have belongs to God. It is part of our worship to give Him a portion of what we have earned. Our Lord daily blesses us with multiple blessings. Although this song is sung as an offertory response, all things come in many forms—health, wealth, time, talents, etc. All means everything, and with a grateful heart we sing this offertory song.

Dear Lord, Thank you, Jesus, for the blessings
you give us. It gives us pleasure to give back to you
for your many blessings. We pray as we monetarily
give back to your church that our monies will be
used for the building of your kingdom. Amen.

Songs Related to All:

1. All Things Come of Thee, O Lord - Ludwig Beethoven
2. All Things Come of Thee, O Lord - John F. Wilson
3. All I Have is Christ - Jordan Kaiflin
4. With All My Heart - Martyn Layzell

Jesus

Philippians 2:10-11

"^{10}That at the name of Jesus every knee should bow, of things in heaven, and things in earth, and things under the earth; ^{11} And that every tongue should confess that Jesus Christ is Lord, to the glory of God the Father."

At birth, everyone is given a name. Every name should have a meaning. God the Father named Jesus. He sent an angel to deliver the message to Mary, the mother of Jesus, of what Jesus' name would be and its meaning. Luke 2:21 tells us, "His name was called Jesus, which was so named of the angel before he was conceived in the womb."

Can you imagine Mary speaking His name after giving birth in the stable? Jesus! The name is so sweet. The mention of Jesus' name sets demons to flight. The mention of His name heals the brokenhearted. Have you called on Jesus when in trouble and He came to your aid? Oh, the name of Jesus. There is no other name above His.

It is shameful that some people disrespect the name of the Jesus by using His name when they are exasperated. The name of Jesus is to be revered. We call on His name in praise, in prayer, in adoration, and in trouble. Jesus is the name above all names.

Dear Lord, Oh, how precious is your name. Jesus! Jesus! Oh, how sweet the name. Jesus! Our Savior, Lord, and King! Jesus, our deliverer! Oh, how precious is your name. We love you, Jesus! Amen.

Songs Related to Jesus:
1. Jesus Name Above All Names - Nadia Hearn
2. Take The Name of Jesus With You (Precious Name) - Lydia Odell Baxter / William Howard Doane
3. Oh, How Precious (is the Name of Jesus) -
Myrna Summers
4. The Name of Jesus is So Sweet - William C. Martin

Lift

Psalm 121:1-2

"[1]I will lift up mine eyes unto the hills, from whence cometh my help. [2]My help cometh from the LORD, which made heaven and earth."

Imagine being in the valley. When you lift up your eyes, beautiful mountains are in view. The psalmist David knew where his help came from. He wrote that he lifted his eyes to the hills. That means he had to make a decision to lift his head and look beyond. It is quite difficult to lift your eyes without lifting your head. As we look to the Lord, we are able to look up from where our help comes from. No one is higher than the Lord. Look up and see God. He is our help.

Samson in Judges 16:28 needed to rely on the Lord for physical strength and help. He asked God for it, and God gave it. Elijah asked God for help when dealing with the Israelites. They needed to choose God over the false prophets of Baal. (1 Kings 18: 21, 32, 37-39)

Cast down? Are our problems, trials, and tribulations getting us down? Is there anything too hard for God?

(Jeremiah 32:27) Trust God to fix it. He knows all about it. Lift your burdens to the Lord in prayer and supplications. Heads up! God is our help! He will fix it! Romans 8:28 states, "And we know that all things work together for good to them that love God, to them who are the called according to his purpose."

Dear Lord, We lift our heads with our eyes on you. Our help and strength come from you. We rely on your help. Your Word says to ask anything in your name. Lord, we need your help. Empower us today to live holy and walk in your way! Amen.

Songs Related to Lift:

1. Lift Up Your Heads Oh Ye Gates - Preashea Hilliard
2. My Help (Cometh From The Lord) -

Jackie Gouche Farris

3. Lift Up Your Heads - Israel Houghton
4. Lift Up Your Heads (anthem) - Emma L. Ashford

Fear Not

Deuteronomy 31:8

"And the Lord, he it is that doth go before thee; he will be with thee, he will not fail thee, neither forsake thee: fear not, neither be dismayed."

Can you imagine hearing the prophet Elijah speak the words from today's scripture? He told the people, not to fear. God's got it!! God will fight for us (Deuteronomy 3:2). Lean and trust His Word. Why did the prophet give the Israelites those words? The people were wavering in their faith. Fear of being destroyed was on their minds. God also told Abraham and Moses not to fear. Many years later, the angel of the Lord told Joseph those exact words—fear not. God was going to take care of him and Mary throughout the journey of the birth of Jesus. A popular acrostic explains fear.

F—False

E—Evidence

A—Appearing

R—Real

(Some use E—Expectation.)

The unknown is very scary, but God knows all about it. Since our scripture today states we should *"fear not, neither be dismayed,"* we must trust God to handle our situations. Quote scriptures and remember how God handled our situations in past times. Remember, we have history with God. We need not be scared. Fear not! Our God is with us.

Dear Lord, We see, hear, and understand the words "Fear not." However, help us, Lord, to believe it and move in the power of your Word when fear comes upon us. Help us to trust and believe that you are in control of our lives. Nothing gets past you. Amen.

Songs Related to Fear Not:
1. Fear Not - Glenn Burleigh
2. How Firm a Foundation (vs. 2) - Unknown
3. Fear Not - Chris Tomlin / Ed Cash
4. No Never Alone (vs. 1) - Eliza E. Hewitt

Fear

Psalm 27:1

"The Lord is my light and my salvation; whom shall I fear?
The Lord is the strength of my life;
of whom shall I be afraid?"

Many people love dogs. However, there are many others who see a dog and immediately become fearful. Some fear what others can do to them. Others fear heights, small rooms, new adventures, and the list goes on, but we should never fear because the Lord is our light and salvation.

Some situations in our lives cause fear because of a possible unwanted negative outcome. The scripture says to not be afraid. The Lord will walk and guide us along any pathway. We need God's light and direction to help us.

Have you ever been in a dark place and needed light to help make the pathway clear? For instance, going to the bathroom during the night without turning the light on to get there. We know the way to the bathroom, but there is always the unknown. For example, a shoe, toy, a piece of paper, or book may be on our path to the bathroom. There is a measure of fear that we can possibly trip over something. Light, which would rid us of that fear or tripping over something, would make the trip to the bathroom less dangerous.

Shall I be afraid? No! Our heavenly Father is here with us. The Lord is our light. He makes the pathway clear. Don't be afraid. Fear is not of God. Trust Him and see the light!

Our Gracious Lord and Father, There are times when we find ourselves in difficult situations and we are afraid. We know to put our trust in you, but we don't. You are our light, our salvation, and strength. We put our trust in you. Amen.

Songs Related to Fear:
1. The Lord Is My Light (Gospel) - Lillian Bouknight
2. The Lord Is My Light (Gospel) - Andrae Crouch
3. The Lord Is My Light (Classical) - Frances Allitsen
4. Everlasting God - William Murphy

Day

Psalm 118:24

"This is the day which the Lord hath made;
we will rejoice and be glad in it."

A year has 365 days (with the exception of leap year). Without exception, the length of each day is 24 hours, beginning at 12:00 AM and ending at 11:59 PM. When the twenty-four hours is over, a new day begins. Who put this all into motion? Who created the night, which turns into morning? Who put the sun in its place? No worldwide governmental committee constructed our days. Our heavenly Father put this in motion when He created the earth. He created the day. God is timeless, though we have organized time. He transcends time and the nature of it.

How many of you have seen the movie *Groundhog Day*? In this movie, each new day started over, just as it did the day before, repeating the events of the previous day. Finally, one day, a brand new day occurred with new events.

The blessing is that if we mess up on a particular day, a new day begins at midnight to try again. Praise God! We can start over. New mercies. New day. New beginnings. We will bless the Lord every day. We will rejoice in it.

Dear Lord, Each day is a new day with new mercies attached to you. Blessings unto you for you wake us up each morning and are with us through each day. Your loving kindness is greater than life. We will rejoice in this day and be glad no matter what the day holds in store for us. When we lose our way, please remind us that this is the day that you have made and to rejoice and be glad. Amen.

Songs Related to Day:

1. This is the Day - Les Garrett

2. All Night All Day - Negro Spiritual

3. Give Us This Day - Edwin Hawkins

4. Days of Elijah - Robin Mark

Light

Matthew 5:16

"Let your light so shine before men, that they may see your good works, and glorify your Father which is in heaven."

The purpose of light is to shine and brighten a space. Children love to sing "This Little Light of Mine." Children understand the message in the song and let their God light shine throughout their home, school, and neighborhood. As adults, this message should continue in every aspect of our lives. Can our neighbors, co-workers, and family members see our light?

Without light, the space is dim or dark. It's difficult to be seen or walk in darkness. Matthew in today's scripture gives us a directive to let our light shine! He also tells us where and why. Our desire is to shine to glorify God, not us. If the spotlight shifts to you, quickly direct it onto God! Let your light shine at all times. Shine for Jesus! Shine every day. Reflect the light of Christ in our lives as we live our lives at work, home, or school each day. When difficult situations arise, our reactions, speech, and behavior should reflect the light of Christ.

Dear Lord, we come to thee asking for help, as we desire to let our light shine for thee among others. We take no glory because it belongs to you. Our prayer is that others may see the light in us pointing to you! Amen.

Songs Related to Light:

1. This Little Light of Mine - Negro Spiritual
2. Let the Lower Lights Be Burning - Philip Bliss
3. Let the Heaven Light Shine on me - Negro Spiritual
                                        (Arr. Roland Carter)
4. Shine - Marlene Jenkins Cooper

The King

Luke 23:2-3

"²And they began to accuse him, saying, 'We found this fellow perverting the nation, and forbidding to give tribute to Caesar, saying that he himself is Christ a King.' ³And Pilate asked him, saying, 'Art thou the King of the Jews?' And he answered him and said, 'Thou sayest it."

Kings Nebuchadnezzar, Uzziah, Ahaz, Jehoshaphat, Solomon, David, Agrippa, and Caesar Augustus were just a few of the kings mentioned in the Bible. They ruled over their nations; some were good, and others were bad. Nonetheless, they were given the power to rule over their territories. Some wanted to take other kings' territories and steal their belongings. Jesus, He is Kings of all Kings.

The kings mentioned in the Bible were very powerful, but none were as powerful as Jesus. Many of them had flaws that affected their reign. Even though King Saul, King David, and King Solomon did mighty things as kings in the Bible, they still fell short and had flaws. Jesus has no flaws, and He is the King of the Jews. The Roman soldiers thought they were being funny and disrespectful when they wrote "King of the Jews" on the placard placed on top of His cross. Others mocked him with the title. They were blinded and did not know that Jesus is King of the Jews and Gentiles alike.

We know the King of kings. He reigns over all. Revelation 17:14 states, "These shall make war with the Lamb, and the Lamb shall overcome them: for he is Lord of lords, and King of kings: and they that are with him are called, and chosen, and faithful." Jesus is the King of kings and Lord of lords. None better; none more powerful. Hail, King Jesus!

Dear Lord, our Savior and King, We exalt you, our King of kings and Lords of lord. We magnify your name, and we lift you up. You reign. Yes, you reign! You reign forever. Our God reigns! Amen.

Songs Related to The King:
1. Take Me To The King - Kirk Franklin
2. Celebrate The King - Ricky Dillard
3. He Is King of Kings - Negro Spiritual
4. Oh Worship The King - Johann M. Haydn / Robert Grant

Refuge

Psalm 46:1

"God is our refuge and strength, a very present help in trouble."

When in trouble, where can you run to for help? We can run straight to Christ Jesus. Refuge for my soul! We can take refuge in the Lord because He promised never to leave or forsake us. God will never leave us alone. In Isaiah 43:2, it states, "When thou passest through the waters, I will be with thee; and through the rivers, they shall not overflow thee: when thou walkest through the fire, thou shalt not be burned; neither shall the flame kindle upon thee." When we pass through dark times and deep waters, He promised to be right there for us. We can take refuge in our Savior. Why, you ask? If we go to friends, family, and strangers, they will fail us and not meet our expectations.

Since the Lord already told us to take refuge in Him, we do not have to ask others. He has the ability, the power, and wherewithal to keep us during our struggles. He is able to keep us from falling too. (Jude 24) God is not only our refuge, but our strength as well. When we are weak, He is strong for us. He is always present. He's never a no-show. God is our refuge and strength. Lean and go to Him.

Dear Lord, So glad we can find refuge in you. Where can we flee? We run to you, O Lord. We can hide and be with you, our refuge and strength. Thanks be to God for this help! Amen.

Songs Related to Refuge:

1. You Oh Lord Are My Refuge - Cheri Keaggy
2. Jesus, Lover of My Soul - Charles Wesley
3. Refuge for My Soul - Ronald King
4. What a Friend We Have in Jesus (vs. 2) -

Joseph M. Scriven / Charles C. Converse

Alone

Hebrews 13:5

"Let your conversation be without covetousness; and be content with such things as ye have: for he hath said, I will never leave thee, nor forsake thee."

Has anyone ever been in a room filled with many people, but felt so alone? Feeling alone has many emotions. Some are depressed from being alone. Others like to spend time alone and are called loners. Whatever the situation, hear the voice of the Lord reminding you with His Word that He will never leave or forsake us.

Can you imagine how Daniel felt in the lion's den with just the hungry lions as his companions? While Job was constantly losing everything, his friends and wife told him to curse God and die. Daniel and Job never lost hope, because they kept their trust in God. Each of them knew God would work it out, and yes, He did! Our Lord and Savior Jesus went to the garden to pray with the disciples, but they fell asleep. The disciples were with him in body only, but not in spirit. Jesus knew God was there with Him as he prepared to embark on his Calvary experience.

We are never truly alone. Others may have forsaken us, or may not emotionally have been there for us, but we have a promise from God that He will never leave us. This is our promise, and God never breaks a promise. His promises are yes and Amen.

Dear Lord, We hear your words spoken by the Apostle Paul, "I will never leave thee, nor forsake thee." We relish in this promise. When we feel alone, we hope to quickly forget, by remembering that your Word states that we are not alone. We are never alone. Amen.

Songs Related to Alone:
1. Lo I Am With You Always - Mollie Carruthers
2. Never Alone - Ludie C. Day Pickett
3. Never Alone (vs. 4) - Philip Percival
                             Simone Richardson

4. Alone - Clint Brown

Love

John 3:16

*"For God so loved the world, that he gave his only
begotten Son, that whosoever believeth in him
should not perish, but have everlasting life."*

Most everyone is looking for love. Many look for love
in the wrong places and in the wrong things. Some people
think they've found love, but it turns out not to be the love
they had in mind. There are three types of love: Eros,
Philos, and Agape. Eros is physical attraction, or romantic
love. Philos is brotherly, or friendly love. Agape is divine,
godly love.

Paul explains and describes true, divine, godly love in
I Corinthians 13. A few of those characteristics of love are
mentioned in verse 4: "Charity [love] suffereth long, and is
kind; charity envieth not; charity vaunteth not itself, is not
puffed up." Agape love is difficult to achieve, but with
God's help, it is attainable. Later in the chapter, Paul states
that, "…It does not dishonor others, it is not self-seeking, it
is not easily angered, it keeps no record of wrongs."
(1 Corinthians 13:6 NIV) We should seek to attain Agape

love in our relationships within the choir, church, home, neighborhood, and at work.

No greater love existed than this. God's love for us was demonstrated on the cross of Calvary. He shed His blood and life on Calvary to pay the price of sin and death on our behalf. There was no greater love than God sending his son to earth to be born a baby, and then become a man to die on the cross for our sins. No greater love!

Dear Father, We are thankful for sending your son to the earth to be the sacrificial lamb that would pay the price for sin and death and give us eternal life. We are also grateful for the love you show to us each and every day. Amen.

Songs Related to Love:
1. Jesus Loves Me This I Know - Anna Bartlett Warner
                                   William B. Bradbury
2. For God So Loved The World - Lanny Wolf
3. No Greater Love - David L. Allen
4. And Can It Be - Charles Wesley / Thomas Campbell

Ready

Luke 12:40

"Be ye therefore ready also: for the Son of man cometh at an hour when ye think not."

Are you ready to walk into Jerusalem just like John or to walk in the promises that God has got for you? Are you ready to forgive those who have hurt you and misused you? Have you decided to do what God told (called) you to do? Have you put your all on the altar? Are you ready to lay your burdens down at the feet of Jesus and /or at the foot of the cross? Are you ready to walk in your anointing? If Jesus came today, are you ready to meet Jesus in the air? Are you ready to do what the Word of God says for every situation?

We are the only ones who can answer the above questions. Are we able to answer all or some of those questions? Our readiness demands our preparation! Our desire should be for the Lord to help us get ready to walk in His way. We want to walk in the path that God has for each us. Get ready! Get ready! Get ready!

Dear Lord, Help us to follow your directives according to your Word! We want to be ready to do your will. If we are not all there, we will encourage each other. Amen.

Songs Related to Ready:

1. Are You Ready For the Coming of the Lord -
                              Ada Ruth Habershon

2. I Wanna Be Ready – (Arr. Rosephanye Powell)

3. Getting Ready To Leave This World - Luther G. Presley

4. Ready To Do His Will - S.E.L. / Charles Davis Tillman

Drink / Thirst

John 6:35

*"And Jesus said unto them, I am the bread of life:
he that cometh to me shall never hunger; and he
that believeth on me shall never thirst."*

The woman at the well met Jesus. He asked her for water. However, He knew she needed the living water. She was baffled by her experience with Jesus, but she knew she wanted never to thirst again. After one drink of the living water, she would never thirst again. The Samaritan woman was at the well because of her thirst. However, she needed the living water as well as water from the well. Jesus asked her for a cup of water, and she gave it to him. After her unusual conversation with Jesus, she knew she wanted the Living Water. Jesus told her He could quench her thirst forever. He is the thirst quencher. He said, "He that believeth on me shall never thirst" (John 6:35).

As Christians, we should hunger and thirst for the Word of God. Drink from the fountain; the fountain that never runs dry. Wells and rivers can dry up. Humans and animals have a basic need to quench thirst. Many try soda, alcohol, lemonade, and juice, but plain water is the satisfier.

Read your Bible. Study His Word. Live it each day. Drink from the fountain; the fountain that never runs dry. Today, people are thirsty. They are looking for the Living Water. Many think they can find satisfaction in a name-brand soda, great wine or champagne, or even a cool glass of water. However, those drinks may quench the thirst for a period of time, but once they have experienced Jesus, the Living Water, they will never thirst again. Let's show others that one drink from the fountain will change their lives. This fountain never runs dry.

Dear Lord, Fill our cup, Lord. Not just our cup, but also the persons who hear our music. People thirst for the true and living God. We constantly want to draw from you, our living fountain. Amen.

Songs Related to Drink:
1. His Name So Sweet - Negro Spiritual
2. I Just Come from the Fountain - Negro Spiritual
3. Come Thou Fount - John Wyeth / Robert Robinson
4. Fill My Cup Lord - Richard Blanchard

Hope

Psalm 39:7

"And now, Lord, what wait I for? My hope is in thee."

At times, some of us lose hope. Why and when do we lose hope? (Pause to reflect.) Could it be because our dreams have not come to pass or maybe our expectations are not met? Have you lost hope? Remember God can see the entire picture. Let Him light the path. Let Him have your hopes, dreams, desires, and expectations.

Our hopes should be built on Jesus Christ and nothing else. Although people put their hope and trust in themselves, others, and things, they will soon fail us. There are many examples in the Bible where putting one's hope in Jesus paid off. Paul and Silas in jail put their hope and trust in Jesus. He delivered them. The woman with the issue of blood put her hope in Jesus and was healed. Where is your hope today? Hope in the Lord at all times. He will never fail!

Dear Lord, Our hope is in you and none other. We put our trust only in you. You will never fail us nor lead us astray. Our hope is in you, O Lord. We wait for direction, instruction, and deliverance for our hope is in you. Amen.

Songs Related to Hope:
1. My Hope Is Built on Nothing Less - Edward Mote
                                            William B. Bradbury
2. The Only Hope We Have Is In Jesus -
                                            Margaret Aikens-Jenkins
3. God Never Fails - George Jordan
4. He Never Failed Me Yet - Robert Ray

Lamp

Psalm 119:105

"Thy word is a lamp unto my feet, and a light unto my path."

Key words in this verse are *feet, light, word, path,* and *lamp.* We are able to walk in the light because the Word of God is light to the pathway we are walking on. Lumen is a measurement of brightness. A 100-Watt bulb gives about 1600 lumens. Most of us know how bright that is. A 100-watt light bulb in a lamp gives off a bright light; its duty is to shine. This light allows our feet and eyes to see where we are and what is around us. We are able to walk without stumbling.

The Word of God is a lamp as well. God's Word allows us to see God's correct path. We can't measure the lumens in the light Jesus gives; it is immeasurable. Nonetheless, we can see because God's light is bright.

Is your path dark and dreary? Do you have questions that have you in the dark? What college should I attend? What job offer should I accept? Should I accept his marriage proposal? Should we purchase this dream home? Go to the Word of God! James 1:5a states "If any of you lack wisdom, let him ask of God." God will make it clear to you. His Word guides our feet.

*Dear Lord, As we read and speak your Word,
the light from your Word shines bright. We pray
that we exude the light that you give in our lives
each day. We pray others may see that light. Amen.*

Songs Related to Lamp:
1. Thy Word Have I Hid in My Heart - Ernest O. Sellers
2. O God of Light - Sarah E. Taylor
3. The Lord is My Light - Lillian Bouknight
4. Give Me Oil in My Lamp - Traditional

Blood

1 John 1:7

"But if we walk in the light, as he is in the light, we have fellowship one with another, and the blood of Jesus Christ his Son cleanseth us from all sin."

What is the purpose of blood in our bodies? Blood carries oxygen throughout our bodies. Blood is the lifeline of a living person. The absence of oxygen in the blood means there is no life. Many senior citizens say that they are blessed to have blood running warm in their veins. Yes! They are right. Blood moving throughout the body is necessary for life, for humans and animals. When our blood is tested or screened by medical personnel, the results can give information about our health dating as far back as three or more months. During certain surgeries, the doctors attach a special blood infusion IV in case blood is lost and must be replenished.

Jesus' blood that was shed on Calvary was necessary to give us eternal life. The result of Jesus' shed blood still applies to our lives more than 2,000 years later. Jesus had to die to pay the penalty for everyone's sin. His blood did not carry oxygen, but gave us eternal life. Jesus' blood saves to the utmost. For there is power in the blood, the blood that Jesus shed for me, and only His blood can save us from our sins. He washed us white as snow with the shedding of blood for us on Calvary.

Dear Lord, Oh, the blood that you shed for us on Calvary. Your blood paid the price of sin and death for our eternal life. We thank you for your sacrifice. Thank you for eternal life. Amen.

Songs Related to Blood:

1. Nothing But The Blood - Robert Lowry
2. Are You Washed In the Blood - Elisha A. Hoffman
3. Oh, the Blood of Jesus - Author Unknown (vs. 1&4)
                               Brenda Barker (vs. 2&3)
4. The Blood Will Never Lose Its Power - Andrae Crouch

Adore

1 Chronicles 29:11

"Thine, O Lord is the greatness, and the power, and the glory, and the victory, and the majesty: for all that is in the heaven and in the earth is thine; thine is the kingdom, O Lord, and thou art exalted as head above all."

Our scripture today does not mention the word adore or adoration in it. However, the author of I Chronicles 29:10 writes about David's prayer unto the Lord and how "David blessed the Lord before the congregation." David speaks of his adoration unto the Lord in his prayer. The Living Bible translation uses the word adore in today's verse.

Adore Him. We adore Him. Who are we speaking about? Jesus! We adore Him as we worship in the sanctuary in song and in words. This five-letter word— adore—holds so much emotion. Synonyms that convey the meaning of adore are exalt, extol, worship, glorify, and reverence. Many of our praise and worship songs use these words to convey our love for Jesus. "We Exalt Thee," "We Worship and Adore You," and "Glorify Your Name" are just three of the thousands of songs that praise and honor our Lord and Savior.

Christian composers have written hundreds of songs based on the word *adore*. Some of these songs are nationally popular, and others are well known in their congregation alone. Does the popularity of a song matter to Jesus? Absolutely not! He receives our adoration, which is not based on the popularity of a song. Jesus does not care if the harmonic structure is correct or the melodic line is easy to sing. He cares about our worship and the condition of our heart. Let's praise, honor, and worship Christ together. O come let us adore Him.

Dear Lord, We adore you. We extol you.
We lift your name on high. Joyfully we adore
you today. You are worthy of our praise. Amen.

Songs Related to Adore:
1. O Come Let Us Adore Him - John Francis Wade
2. Joyful, Joyful, We Adore Thee - Ludwig Beethoven
                                    Henry Van Dyke
3. Holy Father We Adore Thee And All Honor -
                                    E. F. Stewart
4. I Exalt Thee (We Exalt Thee) - Peter Sanchez

Mighty

Job 36:5

"Behold, God is mighty, and despiseth not any:
he is mighty in strength and wisdom."

There is no one mightier than the Lord our God. He is mighty in battle and strength. There are multiple examples of God helping the prophets, kings, and others in the Bible to be successful. One such example is David during his battle against Goliath. This was an unfair match (1 Samuel 17). David was unafraid because he knew God would fight for him.

Each person God helped had to follow His directions and battle plan. Elijah asking God to send fire under the altar is an example of the mighty power of God. In 1 Kings 18, God sent the fire from heaven and "consumed the burnt sacrifice, and the wood, and the stones, and the dust, and licked up the water that was in the trench" (1 Kings 18:38). Our God is mighty in battle. Elijah won the fire battle with the mighty power of God.

God is still mighty in wisdom and strength. What do you need Him to do for you today? There is no reason why we cannot just stop and praise Him for being mighty in wisdom and strength. Yes, we praise you, God, for your mighty acts, wisdom, and strength.

Dear Lord God, You are strong and mighty. You are mighty in wisdom and strength. There is none like you! Amen.

Songs Related to Mighty:

1. Great and Mighty - Marlene Bigley
2. My God is So Big - Ruth Calkin
3. What a Mighty God We Serve - African Folk Song
4. What a Mighty God We Serve - Marcus Dawson

Steven Ford

Lost

2 Corinthians 4:3-4

"[3]But if our gospel be hid, it is hid to them that are lost: [4]In whom the god of this world hath blinded the minds of them which believe not, lest the light of the glorious gospel of Christ, who is the image of God, should shine unto them."

We have the answer for the lost, the perishing, and the unbeliever. We have the blueprint and path to Christ. There is a childhood song that speaks about not hiding "it" under a bushel. We are not to hide the way to Christ from others. It's through the Word of God, our music, and our testimony that others can come to Jesus.

Rescue the lost and perishing. Some people do not know they are lost. Others are seeking and looking for the way to Jesus Christ. Can they find their way? How can they find their way without a preacher? Our music can be the messenger that speaks to the soul and brings the lost to Christ. Consider learning and memorizing Bible verses that give the plan of salvation (i.e., Roman Road, ABC's of Salvation, Four Spiritual Laws). Who knows? Someone may ask you about your salvation and how to obtain what you have. Be ready!

Dear heavenly Father, We come today to ask for assistance with bringing others into the Kingdom of God. Please help some of us who need holy boldness. Let our lives tell the story. Amen.

Songs Related to Lost:

1. Rescue the Perishing - Fanny Crosby

2. Breathe - Michael W. Smith

3. The Shepherd of Love - Albert S. Reitz

4. Love Came Down - Casey Darnell / Ross King
                          Todd Fields / Heath Baltzglier

Morning

Psalm 5:3

"My voice shalt thou hear in the morning, O Lord; in the morning will I direct my prayer unto thee, and will look up."

I rise each morning when the sun rises, signifying a new day and new beginnings. His mercies are new every morning (Ecclesiastes 3:23). Joy comes in the morning too (Psalm 30:5). We can endure the night because the morning is on its way. Trust God because He regulates the morning, noonday, and evening.

There is a variation of minutes from when the sun rises each day according to the time zone one resides in. Most people rise in the morning after a night's sleep, except for those who work the night shift. The sun's job is to light the day and give warmth to the climate, our bodies of water, and the earth. The sun also plays a major role in the process of the water cycle. Who remembers some of these basic scientific facts about the sun? Our God made the sun and all of its properties and functions on the fourth day of creation (Genesis 1:16). Remember, the sun will shine even if you can't feel its rays. In the morning when I rise, great is God's faithfulness.

Dear Lord, In the morning when we rise, you are there. When we go to sleep at night, you are there. We know you are always with us, and we will keep our minds on thee. Amen.

Songs Related to Morning:
1. My Lord, What a Morning - Negro Spiritual
2. Woke Up This Mornin' - Negro Spiritual
3. When Morning Gilds The Skies -

Edward Caswall

4. When I Rose This Morning - Jerry C. Smith

Heaven

John 14:2-3

"²In my Father's house are many mansions: if it were not so, I would have told you. I go to prepare a place for you. ³And if I go and prepare a place for you, I will come again, and receive you unto myself; that where I am, there ye may be also."

Jesus has prepared a place for those who have accepted Him as their personal Savior. Jesus said in John 14:2, "I go to prepare a place for you." Heaven is that place. It's big enough for all those who fit the requirements. There is only one requirement; the person needs to be a Christian, one who is born again.

There is another place prepared by Jesus also called hell. Hell is a real place that was created for those who have rejected Jesus and never accepted Him as their Lord and Savior. Don't you want to go to heaven? Everybody talking about heaven ain't going there. Heaven is a wonderful place. The streets are gold. When we all get to heaven . . . are you in the number? Is your name written in the Lamb's Book of Life? Have you accepted Christ as your personal Savior? We hope to meet you in glory land. When we all get to heaven, we will walk around heaven all day singing, shouting, and praising God. I have my ticket!

(The invitation, plan of salvation, and the Sinner's Prayer begins on page 202.)

Dear Lord, Heaven is our final destination. We will be in heaven with you for eternity. What joy and happiness we will experience just to be at the feet of Jesus! Heaven. We will rejoice in heaven. Amen.

Songs Related to Heaven:

1. When We All Get To Heaven - Eliza Edmunds Hewitt
2. Heaven Is A Wonderful Place - O. A. Lambert
3. Everybody Talkin' 'bout Heav'n Ain't Goin' There -

Negro Spiritual

4. Heaven Came Down - John W. Peterson

Love

Psalm 18:1

"I will love thee, O Lord, my strength."

Psalm 116:1

"I love the Lord, because he hath heard my voice and my supplications."

There are so many reasons why we love the Lord. Today we highlight His willingness to hear us. The Lord is our strength; He hears our voices and supplications. The Lord empowers us with His strength because our strength fails. He hears us when we pray at any time of the day or night. He listens in any language or dialect that we speak from any culture, and we do not need a translator to interpret for us. We do not have to make an appointment or pray at a particular time.

The Lord hears our supplications, petitions, and requests without conditions. The Lord also answers them as well, but as He sees fit. He gives us peace. We do not have to worry because the Lord is there! If the Lord did not do another thing for us, would we love Him anyway? We do not have to worry because He does for us on a consistent basis. His unconditional love empowers us. I love the Lord. We love the Lord. Let all the people praise Him forever and forever.

Dear Lord, We love you today with our whole heart. We love you because you listen and hear our prayers. Knowing that you attend to our requests and petitions comforts us. Finally, the strength that you give holds us up and keeps us going. We love you today! In Jesus' name, Amen.

Songs Related to Love:
1. I Really Love The Lord - Jimmy Dowell
2. Precious Jesus - Thomas A Whitfield
3. I Love You, Lord, Today - William F. Hubbard
4. I Love The Lord - Richard Smallwood

Crown

1 Peter 5:4

"And when the chief Shepherd shall appear,
ye shall receive a crown of glory that
fadeth not away."

After the Second Coming of Jesus, there is the final judgment seat of Christ. It is here where Jesus will give us our crowns. There are different types of crowns. The crown of life (James 1:12), the crown of righteousness (2 Peter 4:8), and the crown of glory (1 Peter 5:4) are just a few. Our verse today states that these crowns will not fade away. After we receive our crowns, we will lay them at the feet of Jesus. I shall wear a crown, but not until the trumpet sounds and Jesus cracks through the sky to take us to heaven.

Be watchful. No one knows the day or the hour that He will appear. We shall see Jesus face to face. Then there is the ceremony in heaven when we receive what is due us. What a time of rejoicing it will be.

Dear Lord, the crowning day is quickly approaching. We know that the crowns we will receive are an extra blessing for the service and life we have lived. Thank you, Jesus. We are not worthy, but we say thanks. Amen.

Songs Related to Crown:
1. I Shall Wear a Crown - Thomas Whitfield
2. The Crown - B.B. Edmiaston / Emmett S. Dean
3. Ain't That Good News - Negro Spiritual
4. Is It the Crowning Day? - Henry Ostrom

Magnify

Psalm 34:3

"O magnify the Lord with me, and let us exalt his name together."

What a blessing it is to be able to magnify, exalt, and praise together as a choir, praise team, or Christian musical group. Together as a music unit, we play our instruments and lift our voices in unison and harmony. What a beautiful sight and sound as our collective purpose in music ministry is to exalt the Lord our God together in our musical offering!

Magnifying and exalting the name of the Lord together as a singing unit is exactly what today's scripture exhorts us to do. Lifting up the name of Jesus in multiple keys, tonalities, harmonies, rhythmic patterns, and sometimes in different languages, gives us the opportunity to praise the Lord in song for His goodness, mercy, excellent greatness, majesty, power, and authority over all. What a mighty God we serve!

Dear Lord, We magnify you today in song and words. We lift our voices and sing the words of adoration. You alone are worthy. We exalt thee and adore thee. We magnify your name! Praises to your Holy name. Amen.

Songs Related to Magnify:

1. O Magnify - Michael D. Popham / Regi Stone
2. Magnify the Lord With Me - Sandra Crouch
3. I Come To Magnify The Lord - Mark Condon
4. My Soul Does Magnify The Lord -
   Babbie Mason / Randy Phillips

Mercy

2 Corinthians 4:1

"Therefore seeing we have this ministry, as we have received mercy, we faint not;"

Who can grant us mercy? Could it be the teacher who grants mercy when our research paper is not handed in on time? Or our parents when we miss the curfew? Could it possibly be the traffic court judge when he throws out the charges against us? We could go on and on. We all want God's mercy. His mercy supersedes all of the above and those too numerous to mention, but the mercy of the Lord frees us a thousand-fold more than any earthly power can.

The title of Margaret Douroux's song "Mercy That Suits" says it all. Mercy suits our case! We can't give ourselves mercy. Someone else must grant it. When we receive mercy, it is not based on anything we have done. God's new mercies are granted to us each new day. The overwhelming goodness of God is that he grants mercy to the just and unjust, and to the saved and unsaved. His mercies are new every morning. Great is God's faithfulness. (Lamentations 3:22-23)

Dear Lord, Please have mercy on your children. We do not deserve it, but need your mercy today. Each of us may need mercy for different reasons. We accept your mercy and say thanks. Amen.

Songs Related to Mercy:

1. Mercy That Suits - Margaret Douroux
2. Great is Thy Faithfulness - Thomas O. Chisholm
William M. Runyan
3. I Will Sing of the Mercies - James Henry Fillmore
4. Requiem - Kyrie Eleison (Lord, Have Mercy) -
Wolfgang Mozart

Serve

Psalm 100:2

"Serve the Lord with gladness: come before his presence with singing."

Is there mental, spiritual, or physical stress in Christian ministry? The struggle is real. Sometimes our family responsibilities, others in ministry, or ourselves cause us to temporarily lose our joy and gladness while ministering to others! Serve the Lord with a joyful heart. Serving the Lord is a privilege and honor. Our service to the Lord should not be a laborious task. Serve the Lord with gladness!

Has there been a time in your music ministry that you had to serve, even when you didn't want to? For instance, when it was 4° or 94° degree weather outside, or two feet of snow, or torrential rains pouring down from heaven? Was the song "I Will Serve Thee," in the key of E*b*, coming from your lips and heart? Sometimes the weather or personal problems may hinder us from serving the Lord with gladness. Nonetheless, God honors our service to Him, and the listeners enjoy our music. Even when the church is half empty due to the weather conditions, our music and message will touch and minister to those in attendance. The icing on the cake is when a parishioner states how the music has blessed them that particular day. We will serve the Lord on any given day, as long as we have breath.

Dear Lord, It is our pleasure to serve you, O Lord. Please accept our music ministry to you. We ask for strength and wisdom as we minister with our brothers and sisters. May we not quickly take offense to the persons we sing with in the choir or play with in the band. Help us be faithful and dependable for your service. Amen.

Songs Related to Serve:
1. I Will Serve Thee - Bill & Gloria Gaither
2. I Give Myself Away - William McDowell
3. It Pays to Serve Jesus - Frank C. Houston
4. O Jesus, I Have Promised - John Ernest Bode
                                    Arthur Henry Mann

Presence

Genesis 3:8

"And they heard the voice of the Lord God walking in the garden in the cool of the day: and Adam and his wife hid themselves from the presence of the Lord God amongst the trees of the garden."

Adam and Eve ran from the presence of God because of the sin they committed. Up until this time, they experienced a great relationship with God in the garden. As soon as they sinned, they experienced a breach in their relationship. They hid and clothed themselves. Previously, Adam and Eve did not know they were naked. Sin changed their relationship with God and caused them to run from His presence. Adam and Eve also discovered their nakedness after they sinned against God.

We should always desire to be in the presence of the Lord, but sin is a barrier to this relationship. Is there anything in our lives that is causing us to run from His presence? Could it be sin, grief, unmet expectations, or disappointment? Read God's Word and meditate on it. Let

God's Word make you whole, clean, and restored. For in the presence of the Lord is joy!

Dear Lord, In your presence is joy. We want to be in your presence. Let us not run from your presence because of sin. We want to be right with you. Amen.

Songs Related to Presence:

1. Here We Are In Your Presence - Dallas Holm
2. The Presence Of The Lord Is Here - Kurt Carr
3. Holy Ground - Geron Davis
4. Oh The Glory Of His Presence - Steve Fry

Victory

1 Corinthians 15:57

"But thanks be to God, who gives us the victory through our Lord Jesus Christ."

Who wants to lose or be a loser in a battle or competitive game? Almost everyone wants to be a winner. We must pick the right team in order to win! Who likes playground picks? Were you the first or the last chosen? If Jesus is on our team and is leading the battle, we are victorious. Jesus is omnipresent! He will be on everyone's team, if only we call Him Lord and want Him on our team. Pick Jesus! Team Jesus here!

We know that we have won before the battle has started. Nonetheless, our flesh sometimes gets weary and we get scared that we will fail. Help! When in trouble, Jesus told us to call on Him and He will answer and show up. (Jeremiah 33:3) In this battle, Jesus is the captain of our team. He will fight the battle for us. The battle's over. We win! Romans 6:37 states, "Nay, in all these things we are more than conquerors through him that loved us." Our enemies have been put down. Jesus has already won it for us. Shout now!

Dear Lord, We are victors in Christ Jesus. Lord, we know the battle is over before it starts. We rely on you! Help us when we get scared when we are in the fight of our lives. We know the battle is yours, but please remind us when we forget. Victory is ours today. Amen.

Songs Related to Victory:

1. Victory In Jesus - Eugene M. Bartlett
2. Victory is Mine - Dorothy Norwood
3. Faith Is The Victory - John Yates / Ira Sankey
4. In The Name of Jesus - Unknown

Shepherd

Psalm 23:1

"The Lord is my shepherd; I shall not want."

This powerful verse is less than ten words, but speaks volumes! These words are easily understood. We shall lack nothing, because He is our shepherd. A shepherd takes care of his sheep. A shepherd's job is to make sure not one sheep is harmed or lost, and is able to eat green grass and drink water. Our heavenly father shepherds us. Isaiah speaks of how Jesus the shepherd will take care of us in Isaiah 40:11. "He shall feed his flock like a shepherd: he shall gather the lambs with his arms, and carry them in his bosom, and shall gently lead those that are with young."

George Frideric Handel, the great 18th-century composer, depicted these same words with a beautiful melody supported by a great orchestral accompaniment in the song, "He Shall Feed His Flock" in his *Messiah* oratorio. Yes, with His rod and staff, the Lord is our shepherd, and he will lead and guide us.

Dear Lord, We need and are grateful for your daily protection and guidance. You are our good shepherd, and we are blessed you care for us. When we go astray, you are there to show us the way. Never alone, because our shepherd is with us. Our shepherd, guide, and protector. Amen.

Songs Related to Shepherd:

1.The Lord Is My Shepherd I'll Not Want -

     W. Whittingham / F. Rous / J. S. Irvine

2. The New 23rd - Ralph Carmichael

3. Saviour like a Shepherd Lead Us -

     Dorothy Ann Thrupp

4. My Shepherd Will Supply My Need - Isaac Watts

New

2 Corinthians 5:17

"Therefore if any man be in Christ, he is a new creature: old things are passed away; behold, all things are become new."

When you hear the word *new,* what comes to mind? Perhaps new walk, new wine (Matthew 9:16), new eyes, new life or creature, new song (Psalm 40:3), new things (Isaiah 43:19), new name (Isaiah 62:2 or Revelation 2:17), new heaven and new earth (Isaiah 65:17), new spirit and new heart (Ezekiel 36:26), new clothes (Matthew 9:17), and new covenant (Hebrews 12:24).

The Bible ends with Revelation 21:5, "And he that sat upon the throne said, Behold, I make all things new. And he said unto me, Write: for these words are true and faithful." Put away the old and take on the new. Jesus makes us brand new!

Dear Lord, You make all things brand new. No one has that power, but you. We want to put off the old, and put on the new. We want to do new things in our lives. We rely on you for help and strength in this area. Amen.

Songs Related to New:

1. I Will Do A New Thing - Audrey Byrd

2. A New Name In Glory - Charles Austin Miles

3. New Life - Carol Antrom

4. I Am New - Jason Gray / Joel Hanson

Communion

Mark 14:22

"And as they did eat, Jesus took bread, and blessed, and brake it, and gave to them, and said, Take, eat: this is my body."

Communion is one of the two ordinances of the church. Communion is often called the Lord's Table, the Lord's Supper, the breaking of bread, and the Eucharist. As Christians, we celebrate and call into remembrance Jesus' death, burial, and resurrection with the Lord's Supper each month. Some churches serve communion every Sunday, twice a month, or once a month. No matter when we take communion, we honor Jesus Christ at the table with the wine (grape juice) symbolizing his blood, and bread (wafer) symbolizing His body. We shall not forget His act of love for us on Calvary.

Leonardo da Vinci, the famous 15th-century Italian painter, painted the famous oil painting entitled *The Last Supper,* displayed in the Convent of Santa Maria delle Grazie in Milan. The painting depicts Jesus' Last Supper with the disciples before going to the cross. The painting is beautiful and is a major work of art. We honor and remember the Lord with the ordinance of communion.

Dear Lord, We remember your act of kindness, sacrifice, and love on Calvary. As we take communion, we remember the blood that was shed for us. We remember the body that was literally broken for us by those Roman soldiers. You were sent to earth to save us all through your death, buriel, and resurrection. Thank you, Jesus. Amen.

Songs Related to Communion:

1. Let Us Break Bread Together - Negro Spiritual
2. Do This In Remembrance of Me - Glenn Burleigh
3. Come To The Table of Grace - Barbara Hamm
4. Break Thou the Bread of Life - Mary A. Lathbury

William F. Sherwin

Cross

Philippians 2:8

*"And being found in fashion as a man, he humbled himself,
and became obedient unto death, even the
death of the cross."*

The wooden cross that Jesus had to carry up the hill for His Crucifixion is a visual picture that possibly resonates in all of our minds. Carrying that cross up the hill added to the pain and agony Jesus had to endure that day. Jesus paid it all on that cross. He bore all of our iniquities, sin, and shame.

How can we repay Him for all He has done and continues to do for us? Worshiping God in spirit and truth, sharing Christ with others, and performing service unto Him are just a few ways to remember His act of love. They hung him high on the cross, stretched his arms from east to west with nails in His hands, gave him vinegar to drink, and mocked Him. He never said a mumbling word. He did it all just for you and me. That's love.

God's love for us was proven when He sent his Son to earth and then died on the cross for our sins. Romans 5:8c states, "While we were sinners Christ died for us." That is love!

Dear Lord, Oh, such love that was shown to us on Calvary. We cannot repay you for what was done for us on that. We give you glory! Amen.

Songs Related to Cross:

1. Calvary - Negro Spiritual
2. Alas! And Did My Savior Bleed (At The Cross) -
   Isaac Watts / Ralph E. Hudson
3. Down at The Cross (Glory to His Name) –
   Elisha Albright Hoffman / Russell Mauldin
4. Just For You and Me - Marlene Jenkins Cooper

Sin

2 Corinthians 5:21

"For he hath made him to be sin for us, who knew no sin; that we might be made the righteousness of God in him."

Sin is transgression against God. Sin is simply when we go against God's rules and His plan for our life. *Sin* is such an ugly word, but the Bible states all have sinned and have come short of the glory of God (Romans 3:23) Therefore, none of us are exempt from committing sin, though we are not to look for opportunities to transgress God's laws. When sin comes into our lives, come to Jesus and ask for forgiveness (1 John 1:9). We never want to keep unconfessed sin abounding in our lives. Unconfessed sin affects our prayer life and our walk with Christ. (Psalm 66:18) Sin also affects and will hinder our music ministry. Jesus paid the price so that we could have eternal life.

David spent an entire chapter explaining his sorrow over the sin in his life in Psalm 51. He asks for mercy, to be washed from his iniquity, cleansed from his sin, restoration of the joy of his salvation, given a clean heart, and a renewed right spirit. Can you feel his pain? David was granted his wishes. Let no sin reign in our bodies! (Romans 6:12)

> *Dear Lord, We are sorry for those things that don't please and honor you. Sin has no place in our lives. Thanks for taking our sins upon you on the cross and cancelling the penalty of sin. Amen.*

Songs Related to Sin:
1. Yield Not To Temptation - Horatio R. Palmer
2. It is Well With My Soul (vs. 2) - Horatio G. Spafford
   Philip P. Bliss
3. Nothing But The Blood (vs. 1) - Robert Lowry
4. Though Your Sins Be As Scarlet - Fanny Crosby

Holy

Isaiah 6:3

"And one cried unto another, and said, Holy, holy, holy, is the Lord of hosts: the whole earth is full of his glory."

The words "holy, holy, holy" are mentioned in succession as such, twice in the King James Version of the Bible. Only God is holy. In our verse today, Isaiah talks about the holiness of God and how the earth is full of his glory. Four beasts in the book of Revelation speak of the holiness of God, "Holy, holy, holy, Lord God Almighty, which was, and is, and is to come." (Revelation 4:8) Only God is holy. No one else compares to him. He is worthy to receive glory, honor, and praise.

When we minister in an instrumental offering, song, or the dance, our songs should give God all the glory, honor, and praise he alone deserves. May we never try to take any of God's honor, glory, and praise. We reverence the Lord our God. We worship him in all of His glory. There is none like him. "Holy, holy, holy, Lord God Almighty." (Revelation 4:8)

Dear God our Father, We recognize your
holiness and greatness. We know there is none
like you. We worship and adore you. You alone are
worthy of all the honor, glory, and praise. Amen.

Songs Related to Holy:

1. Holy, Holy, Holy - Reginald Heber

2. Holy, Holy, Holy - Gary Oliver

3. Only You Are Holy - Donnie McClurklin

4. Holy, Holy - Jimmy Owens

Nobody

2 Corinthians 12:11 (NASB)

"I have become foolish; you yourselves compelled me.
Actually I should have been commended by you, for in no
respect was I inferior to the most eminent apostles,
even though I am a nobody."

Paul speaks about being a nobody. After all his works among the people, the people still thought he was a nobody. Sometimes people see us as nobodies as well. But God sees us as someone! We are valued. We have great worth. It is not what people say about us. It is what we say about ourselves.

It's true that there is nobody greater than God, but God sees us as precious in His sight. We are special to Him. Would God send his son to earth for nobodies? Absolutely not! God loved us so much that He sent His son to die for us.

We can be in a crowd of 1,000 or a crowd of ten and possibly not be seen. But God sees and hears us. We matter in His sight. We are somebody in His eyes. Don't worry about how others see us. Know that God sees and deems us valuable and a somebody.

Dear Lord, We recognize that nobody can do what you do or have done! Nobody can take our sins away, heal the sick, raise the dead, intervene in the circumstances in our lives for good, know how we truly feel, know our struggles and know how to fix them, grant us eternal life, etc. Nobody but you, Lord. You only! Amen.

Songs Related to Nobody:

1. Nobody But You Lord - Norman Hutchins
2. Nobody Greater - Vashawn Mitchel
3. Nobody Knows But Jesus - Robert M. Offord
4. Nobody Knows The Trouble I've Seen - Negro Spiritual

Testimony

Luke 21:13

"And it shall turn to you for a testimony."

Psalm 119:31

"I have stuck unto thy testimonies: O Lord,
put me not to shame."

In the word *testimony* resides the word *test*. A student of study may attest to the fact there are different categories of tests. There are easy, difficult, and fun tests. Nonetheless, we must take the test. It is our desire to pass the test in our lives with flying colors. On some tests, we will not do our best due to certain circumstances. Those circumstances must be removed when that test comes around again.

Remember those spelling tests in grade school, when we exchanged tests so that our neighboring classmate could correct our mistakes? In life, our friends and family watch as we take our life's test. Some are there to help us do better the next time, and others criticize quietly or loudly. No matter what the circumstance, we have to take all kinds of tests. Tests allow us to assess if we know the information and can use it properly. Do not be afraid. Take the test! Our testimonies will be better for it.

Dear Lord, My testimony is to live for thee! My life, actions, and songs are living testimony to the God I worship and adore. We want our test to glorify you no matter if we pass or fail. But, we want to pass the test that is given to us. May you be glorified through our trials, test, and our testimony. Amen.

Songs Related to Testimony:

1. I Got A Testimony - Anthony Tidwell
2. Jesus Is Real To Me - Beatrice Brown
3. All The Way My Savior Leads Me - Fanny Crosby
4. And Can It Be - Charles Wesley

Emmanuel

Matthew 1:23

"Behold, a virgin shall be with child, and shall bring forth
a son, and they shall call his name Emmanuel,
which being interpreted is, God with us."

The Jews were anxiously waiting for the Messiah. However, they did not recognize Him when he came. God sent His son to the earth. God named Him Emmanuel. The angel told Mary that His name would be called Emmanuel, meaning "God with us."

We know who the Messiah is. He came as a baby and fulfilled His mission while on earth for thirty-three years. He died for our sins, rose again, and later ascended into heaven. And now we are waiting for His return. O Come, O Come, Emmanuel. We are waiting for your return. He will crack the sky and come for His children.

However, there are many people who do not know who Emmanuel is. We must tell them! We can tell them through our music, our lives, and our conversations with them. How will they who do not know about Christ learn who He is? We must tell them. Go and share Emmanuel with others.

Dear Lord, God you are with us every day, every minute of the hour. You sent your son to be with us and pay for our sins on Calvary, then you sent your Holy Spirit to be a comfort to us. God the Father, Son, and Holy Spirit, we are blessed to call ourselves your sons and daughters. Amen.

Songs Related to Emmanuel:
1. Emmanuel - Norman Hutchins
2. O Come O Come Emmanuel - John Mason Neale
3. Emmanuel, Emmanuel - Bob McGee
4. His Name Is Called Emmanuel - Ken Bible

Tom Fettke

Teach

John 8:2

"And early in the morning he came again into the temple, and all the people came unto him; and he sat down, and taught them."

Jesus, the rabbi, minister, and teacher, taught in the synagogues and to groups of people. Many people listened. Others listened to His teachings to foolishly ask questions, and others listened to get knowledge and answers. The scribes and Pharisees had so many questions. But did they really want answers? There were so many others who wanted to listen to Jesus. A teacher's job is to impart knowledge to the students and listeners. These people in the Bible were hungry for the knowledge and teachings of Jesus. Are we as hungry as those people?

We glean knowledge and insight as we read the Bible and hear the Word of the Lord. Many times when we read the Bible, we receive a Word from the Lord at an impertinent time or moment in our lives. In John 14:26, John said, "He shall teach you all things and bring all things to your remembrance." (The Holy Ghost, which is a

140

part of the triune God, does the same.) It is recorded later in John 8:30 that, "As he spake these words, many believed on him."

Do we believe? We will sing your Word that others may come to the saving knowledge of Jesus.

Dear Lord, Yes Lord, we believe. Please help us with our faith. We know your truths and words are recorded in your Word! We believe. When we forget, please remind us of the words written in the Bible. Please plant your words in our hearts. Amen.

Songs Related to Teach:
1. Savior, Teach Me, Day by Day - Jane Elizabeth Leeson
2. Teach Me Thy Way, O Lord -

Benjamin Mansell Ramsey
3. Teach Me Thy Will, O Lord - William M. Runyan
4. Teach Me - Victor H. Benke / Kate Ulmer

Hope

Psalm 31:24

"Be of good courage, and he shall strengthen your heart, all ye that hope in the Lord."

Why is it sometimes difficult for us to put our hope and trust in God, and choose to put it in earthen vessels? When do we lose hope? (Think and reflect.) Do we lose hope when our dream dies, or when we fail, or when our expectations are not met? When there is no possible way for a great outcome, is our faith, hope, and trust still in God?

When the road and journey looks bleak, keep your hand in God's hand. Ask Him to help you when your faith and hope wavers. He will strengthen and keep you because He is able to do it. Psalm 31:4 states "Be of good courage, and he shall strengthen your heart, all ye that hope in the Lord." Friends, family members, and others want to help and mean well with their platitudes, suggestions, and words of encouragement, but remember God knows the plans that He has for you. He has the master plan for your entire life. (Jeremiah 29:11)

142

When our hope wavers, go to the examples of people in the Bible who had to put their hope in God. Remember past experiences where our hope in God took care of the situation. We ought to put our hope in the Lord at all times. God can see the entire picture. Let Him light the path. Let Him have your dreams, desires, and expectations. Hope in the Lord!

Dear Lord, Our hope is in You. There is no other. Our hope is you. So glad you care about us. Amen.

Songs Related to Hope:

1. My Hope is Built (The Solid Rock) - Edward Mote

William B. Bradbury

2. Hope In Me - Martha Munizzi / Mary Alessi

3. The Only Hope We Have - Margaret Aikens-Jenkins

4. His Eye Is On The Sparrow - Charles H. Gabriel

Civilla Durfee Martin

Wonderful

Isaiah 9:6

"For unto us a child is born, unto us a son is given: and the government shall be upon his shoulder: and his name shall be called Wonderful, Counsellor, The mighty God, The everlasting Father, The Prince of Peace."

Many persons feel that these words from the book of Isaiah are very powerful. George F. Handel felt the same when he set them to music in his *Hallelujah Chorus*. When choristers sing the words *Wonderful, Counsellor, The mighty God, The everlasting Father, The Prince of Peace*, the instrumental parts are full of energy and rapid notes.

Beethoven set the names of God to music as well in his "Hallelujah Chorus from the Mt. of Olives." To say these words and have powerful melodies and rhythmic patterns attached to them is awesome! Did Handel and Beethoven know the depth of each of the names of God? Their music sure accentuated who God is.

Let us sing of the God of our universe who is wonderful, the great Counselor, the only mighty God, the everlasting Father, and the Prince of Peace. Can we go on? He is the Lily of the Valley, Bright Morning Star, Alpha and Omega, Rose of Sharon, Jehovah, Elohim, and El Shaddai. Hallelujah!

Dear God our Father, You have so many names to depict who you are. Only you have these names. We bless and honor you today. Amen.

Songs Related to Wonderful:
1. Wonderful Counselor - Negro Spiritual
2. Cornerstone - Leon Patillo
3. Hallelujah Chorus - George F. Handel
4. So Many Wonderful Things About Jesus - F. C. Barnes

Janice Brown

Anything

Jeremiah 32:27

"Behold, I am the Lord, the God of all flesh: is there any thing too hard for me?"

Anything means anything. There is nothing that can trump or surpass anything. God can do anything. In our finite minds, we may think God has failed us on a particular issue or problem in our lives, but we have finite thinking. Remember to trust God that He has everything in control in our lives, world, and our daily living. God is omniscient, which is all knowing. He is omnipotent, which is all-powerful. He is omnipresent, which is everywhere.

It's wonderful that many children are taught this truth at an early age in songs like, "God Can Do Anything But Fail" and "My God Is Big." As we may know, music plays such an indelible part in everyone's life. Isn't it good to know that our children are learning these truths early in life? Now, as adults, we should continue to remember that our God can do anything, but fail. Even if the circumstances are insurmountable, God can do anything but fail. Watch Him work His plan, promises, and see His power!

Dear Lord, We trust in you. Our peace, trust, lives, and dependence is in you. Our Heavenly Father can do anything but fail. We love that confidence in you. With your power and strength, we can do anything too. Amen.

Songs Related to Anything:
1. God Can Do Anything But Fail - Ira Stanphill
2. Perfect Peace - Marlene Jenkins Cooper
3. My God is Big (Great) - Ruth Harms Calkin
4. Anything, Lord, For Thee - E. E. Williams

H. L. Gilmour

Supply

Philippians 4:19

"But my God shall supply all your need according to his riches in glory by Christ Jesus."

His Word states that God will supply all of our needs. The key word is *need*. The scripture doesn't say He will supply all of our wants. However, our heavenly Father does give us some of our wants. We can live without our wants. God knows what we need. We can depend on Him to be our supplier. He is a God that doesn't lie! There are numerous examples of Jesus supplying what people needed in the Bible.

Daniel needed safety from the lions. (Daniel 6: 19- 22) Elijah needed food, and the widow at Zarephath shared her food with him. (I Kings 17: 7-16)   The Hebrew boys, Meshach, Shadrach, and Abed-Nego, needed their God who would sustain them in the midst of the fire, and He did. (Daniel 1) The woman with an issue of blood for needed healing and received it. (Luke 8: 43-48) Paul and Silas in jail needed a rescuer and were let out of jail. (Acts 16) Did Jesus not do it for all these people mentioned here?

"Won't He do it?" What do we have need of today from the Lord? Can you remember how God supplied your needs in the past? Jehovah Rapha, God provides!

Dear Lord, We bless you today. With humble hearts, we are grateful for your many blessings you have bestowed upon each of our families, our church, and us. Thanks for supplying all of our needs. Amen.

Songs Related to Supply:

1. God Will Supply - Kirk Franklin

2. God Will Provide - Olanda Draper

3. He'll Meet My Need (God Will Supply) – Carol Antrom

4. Wherefore Are Ye Doubting and Fearing (chorus) -

Lelia (Mrs. C.H.) Morris

Greater

1 John 4:4

"Ye are of God, little children, and have overcome them:
because greater is he that is in you, than he
that is in the world."

There is no one greater than the Lord our God. And we have God in us because we are children of the King. God is in us. Let us not forget this. In the deep trenches of life, these simple facts sometimes leave us or are hidden from our memory.

Our God is greater, bigger, and stronger than any other. Elijah gave a visual picture of the power of God to Ahab and the followers of Baal on Mt. Carmel. The gods of Baal could not produce fire upon the altar upon which the bullock lay. Elijah's God lit the water-drenched altar with fire under the bullock. This is only one instance of the mighty power of God shown to people.

The Devil, who is in the world, would like to think he is greater than God, and even told Jesus that while on a high mountain. Satan tried to tempt Jesus. "Then saith

Jesus unto him, Get thee hence, Satan: for it is written, Thou shalt worship the Lord thy God, and him only shalt thou serve." (Matthew 4:10)

We must never forget who we belong to. Our family line is greater than any other. We are children of the King. Walk in royalty, power, and strength. No one is greater than our God. No one.

Dear Lord, No one is greater than you, dear Lord. Others have tried to be greater than you, but failed. There is no one greater than you. We worship and adore you. Amen.

Songs Related to Greater:

1. Greater is He That Is In Me - Lanny Wolfe

2. Grace greater than all our Sin - Daniel Brink Towne

Julia Harriett Johnston

3. Nobody Greater - VaShawn Mitchell

4. Amazing Grace (My Chains Are Gone) - Chris Tomlin

John Newton / Louie Giglio

Calvary

Luke 23:33

"And when they were come to the place, which is called Calvary, there they crucified him, and the malefactors, one on the right hand, and the other on the left."

Jesus was crucified at Calvary. The cross of Calvary where Jesus Christ died for our sins is a depiction of love, sacrifice, and redemption. The pain Jesus experienced on the cross on that day was excruciating, but it was necessary for our redemption. He bore our iniquities and transgressions, and freed us from the penalty of sin. Jesus hung on the cross, bled and died, and rose again on the third day. Jesus sacrificed His life for ours. He paid it all at Calvary. No one else was qualified to save us. He was born to die for our sins.

Singing about what Christ did on the cross—enduring the pain, securing our redemption from sin—is heartwarming. He paid it all on Calvary. We should never forget the price Jesus paid for our redemption.

Dear Father, Calvary. Calvary. We are grateful you sent your only son Jesus to die on the cross for our sins at Calvary. We needed a redeeming act, and Jesus did it for us on the cross. Glory to your name! Amen.

Songs Related to Calvary:

1. Calvary - Negro Spiritual
2. At Calvary - Daniel Brink Towner
   William Reed Newell
3. At The Cross (Alas, and did my Savior Bleed) -
   Isaac Watts

4. For My Liberty – Carl Preacher

Satisfy

Psalm 91:16

"With long life will I satisfy him, and shew him my salvation."

Jesus satisfies. He quenches our thirst for the living water. He satisfies our needs and gives us a sense of belonging, as we are His children. Jesus gives us the assurance that we will meet Him in Heaven for eternity. Our souls yearn for someone who can satisfy, and His name is Jesus!

It is our joy and honor to live the life Jesus wants us to live. May He be satisfied with us. It will be great to hear our Lord say, "Well done, good and faithful servant; thou hast been faithful over a few things, I will make thee ruler over many things: enter thou into the joy of thy lord" (Matthew 25:23).

Dear Lord, We have longed for someone to satisfy us. We are satisfied with you. We now know only you can satisfy. We pray for our family and friends who do not know the satisfaction they can have in you. Amen.

Songs Related to Satisfied:

1. Satisfied (All My Life Long I Have Panted) -
                    Clara Tear Williams / Ralph E. Hudson
2. Satisfied With You - Andy Park
3. I'm Satisfied With Jesus - James Cleveland
4. I'm Satisfied With Jesus - Luther Barnes

Rock

Psalm 95:1

"O come, let us sing unto the Lord: let us make a joyful noise to the rock of our salvation."

Have you ever been in the garden and had to move a huge rock? Was it difficult to move? The word rock has been mentioned in the Bible over 125 times. There are also several references made to Jesus being the rock of my salvation. David states in II Samuel 22:4, "The Lord is my rock" He further states in verse 47, "The Lord liveth; and blessed be my rock; and exalted be the God of the rock of my salvation."

Strength, immoveable, strong, and foundational are characteristics of a rock. Jesus possess these characteristics as well. Jesus is our rock, the rock of our salvation. Our hope is in Jesus. He never changes. He is unmovable, but He can move anything that is in our way. He is strong and able. Yes, we will hope in the Lord. We will call Him and go to the rock of our salvation. The rock is Jesus! None other like Him.

Dear Lord, Our trust and hope is in you, the
rock of our salvation. We need you every minute of
the day. Knowing that you are strong and able to
handle each facet of our lives, we put our trust in
you. Amen.

Songs Related to Rock:

1. He Hideth My Soul - Fanny Crosby

                            William J. Kirkpatrick

2. I Go To The Rock - Dottie Rambo

3. I Will Call Upon The Lord (Hosanna, Blessed Be The Rock) (Oh, Magnify the Lord) – Michael O'Shields

4. My Hope is Built (The Solid Rock) –

                    Edward Mote / William B. Bradbury

Listen

Proverbs 1:5

"A wise man will hear, and will increase learning; and a man of understanding shall attain unto wise counsels:"

How does one hear or listen to the voice of God? We hear His voice through scripture, sermons, devotionals, through other Christians, circumstances, Christian songs, and through conversational prayer with Him. The Holy Spirit speaks to our heart as we meditate on the Word of God and pray. Be still! Often times we are too busy to hear what God has to say to us. Try sitting still for ten minutes after a personal devotional time or time of prayer. This is extremely difficult, but it is essential to discipline ourselves to hear the voice of the Lord. The Lord wants to speak to us, but are we listening? Do we have the time and patience to hear from the Lord?

Has there been a time when we did not return a phone call and the information we need was in that phone call? "Call and I will answer thee," says the Lord. He continues on and says, "I will show you great and mighty things."

(Jeremiah 33:3) Listen! Be quiet and still. Hear the words and voice of the Lord.

When the voice of the Lord is heard, do we heed the words of the Lord? Do we obey His words and directions? Do not just call Him—listen and obey when the Lord answers. Heed the words of the Lord!

Dear Lord, Please teach us to listen for your still small voice. Lead us, guide us; help us to learn to listen. Many times we want to talk, talk, talk, ask, ask, ask, complain, complain, complain, but help us to learn to listen for your still small voice of encouragement, direction, guidance, and comfort. Yes, Lord. Amen.

Songs Related to Listen:
1. Listen To The Lambs - Negro Spiritual
2. Listen, God is Calling - Traditional Tanzanian Tune
                                      Harold S. Olson (translator)

3. We Are Listening - Steven Curtis Chapman
4. Listen - Wendell Haynes / Tracy Chapman
                          Kingsley Gardner

Temptation

1 Corinthians 10:13

"There hath no temptation taken you but such as is common to man: but God is faithful, who will not suffer you to be tempted above that ye are able; but will with the temptation also make a way to escape, that ye may be able to bear it."

Quickly think of three songs that speak of temptation or sin that are in our repertoire. (Pause.) There are not many songs that talk of temptation and sin. Some ministers shy away from preaching and talking about it, too. However, we know temptation and sin exist. What are the definitions of each of these words? Temptation is where the presence of sin is for the taking. Sin is transgression against God. Temptation is not sin! Temptation is not sin until we yield to it.

When temptation arises, do not flirt with it. Run! Flee! Resisting temptation often shows us where our heart is and where our spiritual walk is with Christ. When a situation arises that makes us feel the need to lie, stop and do not let the lying words come from your lips. But in case the lying words come out, repent and ask Jesus to forgive you. (I John 1:9)

Many people in the Bible had trouble resisting temptation—Adam, Eve, David, and Samson, to name just a few. However, Joseph resisted temptation in a powerful way. Satan tried to tempt Jesus, but Jesus does not sin. Did Satan know that? Temptations will always be present, but it is advisable to be strong enough to resist! Pray when temptation arises, join support groups, flee, and stay away from situations that bring on temptation.

Dear Lord, It is our desire to live holy and righteous. When sin enters our lives, we will confess. When temptation arises, we will flee. This is our desire, but we do miss the mark at times. We need your help to stay on the right course. Amen.

Songs Related to Temptation:
1. Yield Not To Temptation - Horatio R. Palmer
2. What A Friend We Have In Jesus (vs. 2) -
           Charles C. Converse /Joseph M. Scriven
3. The Lord's Prayer - Albert Hay Malotte
4. He Looked Beyond My Faults - Dottie Rambo

Promise

2 Corinthians 1:20

"For all the promises of God in him are yea, and in him Amen, unto the glory of God by us."

If God promised it in His Word, then it is done! God keeps His promises. As friends, parents, spouses, employers, employees, ministry workers, and so on, we sometimes promise others that we will complete a task, or state that our word is our bond, but fail miserably and don't follow through. We have good intentions, but due to circumstances beyond our control or our own mess-ups, we fail. Jesus never, never fails. His promises always come true.

Some Bible scholars speak about the seven promises if you follow Jesus, the 200 promises Jesus made to mankind, and seven promises God made to man. No matter what number you subscribe to, promises have been made to us by God: Everlasting life if you accept Christ as your Savior (John 3:16). A place in Heaven for believers in Christ (John 14:1). If we confess our sins, He will forgive us (I John 1:9). These are but a few examples. Hold on to the promises! Quote the scriptures. His promises are yes and amen. God keeps His promises!

Dear Lord, Your promises, O Lord, are written on our hearts. We hold dear to the words of your promises. Your promises are yes and amen. Thank you Jesus. Amen.

Songs Related to Promises:

1. His Promises - Carol Antrom
2. I Know God Promises To Be True - Lelia Morris
3. Standing On the Promises of Christ My King - Russel Kelso Carter
4. God Keeps His Promises - Sarah Moore

Call

Psalm 18:3

"I will call upon the Lord, who is worthy to be praised: so shall I be saved from mine enemies."

We will call upon the Lord! Why? Because He is worthy to be praised! And? The Lord will save us from our enemies because He has the power to do so. We possibly have friends who will stand with us against our enemies, but our God is greater than anyone. He will shield us with the breastplate of righteousness and the shield of faith. He will place the helmet of salvation on our head. He will protect us! (Ephesian 4:14) Who else can do all this? Do any names come to mind?

There is a famous line in the movie *Ghostbusters* that states "Who you gonna call?" No! We are not calling the Ghostbusters nor any Superheroes. We will call on the Lord! He is able, powerful, and greater than any other.

When you want to talk to Jesus, there are no phone numbers to memorize, no data rates applied, no busy signals, and no dead cell phone tower zones. So, who you gonna call?

Hear our prayer, Oh Lord. We are blessed that we can call on you in the morning, at noontime, in the evening, and at midnight. We can call you twenty-four hours a day, seven days a week. We are so grateful for the access to your throne. Amen.

Songs Related to Call:
1. I Will Call Upon The Lord - Antwuane Davis
                                Kevin Davidson
2. Call Him Up (Can't Stop Praising His Name) -
                    Herman Netter / Rickey R. Grundy
3. Softly and Tenderly Jesus Is Calling -
                    Will Lamartine Thompson
4. Jesus On the Mainline - Traditional

Lift

John 12:32

"And I, if I be lifted up from the earth, will draw
all men unto me."

Lift Him up! Who do we lift up? We lift up Jesus! The Bible states if we lift Jesus up, He will draw men to the kingdom. Jesus alone deserves all the praise and the glory. There is none like Him. Our beautiful voices, playing instruments, or praise dancing doesn't bring people to Christ. It's the message of Jesus in our music ministry.

While in ministry, we should be careful not to lift ourselves up, exalt the preacher, or give undue praise to any other ministry workers. The focus is always to be on Jesus. The scripture is clear! If we lift Jesus up, He will draw all men unto Him. This is our goal! We want men, women, and children to come to Jesus!

It is Jesus who deserves all the honor and the glory. Lift up Jesus with our lives, hands, praise, actions, and our ministry in song. Lift Him up! Lift Him higher and higher.

Draw all men unto Him. Let's lift up Jesus. Jesus deserves all the praise. Yes, let's lift Him up!

Dear Lord, Father, we lift you up today. It is only you who deserve the praise, glory, and honor. Help us never to take your glory or your praise from you. Our flesh gets weak at times and the praises of men feel good. We honor and lift you up today. We want to draw others to you. Thank you, dear Father, for being the God that you are. Amen.

Songs Related to Lift:
1. Lord I Lift Your Name On High - Rick Founds
2. Lift Him Up - Johnson Oatman
3. High and Lifted Up - Joe Pace
4. Lift The Savior Up - Joe Pace

Peace

Isaiah 26:3

"Thou wilt keep him in perfect peace, whose mind is stayed on thee: because he trusteth in thee."

Mental illness is a serious issue in our world today. Some people are getting help with their illness, while others are untreated or not taking their medicine. Mental illness knows no age, gender, or nationality. Professional help is usually needed to help persons with their mental troubles.

Others suffer from a lack of peace because of the troubles in their life. No peace in our mind can possibly turn into mental illness. Some persons have lost their minds due to major troubles, grief, terrible situations, and the like. But our God gives peace. We are not to dismiss professional help, but God alone can only handle some of our situations.

If you are going through a terrible life event, God grants peace. His Word says so. We must keep our minds on Him. This is not always easy, because of the variables and things happening around us. John 10:10 states, "The thief cometh not, but for to steal, and to kill, and to destroy." The devil wants to steal your joy and peace. Please do not give it to him. But we must go back to the Word of God. He will keep us in perfect peace. "Thou wilt keep him in perfect peace, whose mind is stayed on thee: because he trusteth in thee" (Isaiah 26:3).

Oh Lord, our Lord, We come to you today to bring peace to our situation. You alone know what is going on in our lives. Let us not go crazy with worry or dysfunction. Help us to keep our mind focused on you. Amen.

Songs Related to Peace:
1. Peace, Be Still - Mary A. Baker / H. R. Palmer
2. It is Well With My Soul - Daniel Sidney Warner
                                          Eugene M. Bartlett
3. Perfect Peace - Marlene Jenkins Cooper
4. I've Got Peace Like A River - Negro Spiritual

Joy

Psalm 71:23

"My lips will shout for joy when I sing praise to you."

One of the earliest childhood songs many youngsters learn in Sunday School or Vacation Bible School is "I've Got the Joy, Joy, Joy, Joy Down in My Heart" by George Willis. Children often sing this song with gusto, vitality, and much glee, especially when they get to verse 2, which talks about the devil sitting on a tack if he doesn't like the joy they possess! When children sing, their expressions and movements often are exuberant.

As adults, let us not lose the same joy that Jesus gave us when we accepted Him as our personal Savior. Life experiences, trials, and tribulations will try to steal our joy if we let them, but remember that we have Jesus' joy. We have the joy that only comes from knowing Jesus Christ as our personal Savior. Only Jesus can give us true joy. Sing with Joy!

Dear Lord, We thank thee for the joy that only Jesus gives. Help us to renew this joy on a daily basis. We trust that the congregation or the listeners of our music will experience the joy of Jesus and the joy in our music. We pray that those who are hurting and are not experiencing Jesus' joy will soon experience it or find it once again. In Jesus' name, Amen.

Songs Related to Joy:

1. Joyful Joyful We Adore Thee - Ludwig Beethoven
   Henry Van Dyke
2. I've Got the Joy, Joy, Joy, Joy Down in My Heart -
   George Willis
3. Joy - Kirk Franklin
4. Unspeakable Joy - Douglas Miller

Truth

John 8:32

"And ye shall know the truth, and the truth shall make you free."

Romans 6:23 speaks about the penalty of death being paid for through the death and resurrection of Jesus Christ. However, although Christ paid the debt, we are not free from the bondage of sin unless we accept Jesus Christ as our Lord and Savior. People bound by sin are not free, and they are in a horrible state. Some of them know this to be true, while others do not.

When Jesus frees a person, there is a feeling that is purely unexplainable. The scales drop from the eyes, and the eyes are open to the truth. What is truth? Truth is knowing who Jesus is, knowing what He has and will do for His children, and believing the Word of God.

Some people are very religious and believe they are serving the true and living God. A religious person loves God and believes there is a God. To be religious is not the definition of a Christian. Christians have accepted Christ as their personal Savior. Knowing this truth sets a person free. Let the truth set you free.

Dear Lord, Knowing who you are and accepting you as our Savior sets us free. We are glad we know the truth. Lord, we pray that others may find and know the truth as we do. Amen.

Songs Related to Truth:

1. I'm Free - Percy Bady / Pete Townshend

2. Open My Eyes, That I May See - Clara H. Scott

3. We Worship You (Spirit and In Truth) -

William Murphy III

4. There is Power In the Blood - Lewis E. Jones

Name

Revelation 2:17

"He that hath an ear, let him hear what the Spirit saith unto the churches; To him that overcometh will I give to eat of the hidden manna, and will give him a white stone, and in the stone a new name written, which no man knoweth saving he that receiveth it."

What is in a name? Do people really give thought to the naming of their newborn babies? Every name should have a meaning attached to it. God named Jesus Emmanuel, which means God with us. God sent His Son to the earth as an extension of Him. God with us. God took on the form of a man, Jesus, to live amongst us. God decided to change some people's names in the Bible. Abram was changed to Abraham, which means father of many nations. (Genesis 17:5) Sarai was renamed Sarah, which means mother of nations. (Genesis 17:16) Jacob was changed to Israel, which signifies power with God and men (Genesis 32:28) God changed others too. God wanted a name to show their new position or identity.

When we reach heaven, God will give us our new names. We will receive a new name in glory. The Negro slaves sang a song entitled "I've Got A New Name in Glory." They knew that when they reached heaven they would receive a new name and identity. They knew it would not be one of a slave, either. When we all get to heaven, we will receive new names and new bodies!

Dear Lord, Your name is so sweet. When your name is spoken, demons flee. The power of your name is almost unexplainable. Our words can do so little to try to explain who You are. You mean so much to us. We call on Your name, Jesus! Amen.

Songs of Related to Name:
1. His Name So Sweet - Negro Spiritual
2. In The Name of Jesus - Unknown
3. There's Something About That Name - Bill Gaither
Gloria Gaither
4. I've Got A New Name - Negro Spiritual

Rejoice (in the dance)

Jeremiah 31:13

*"Then shall the virgin rejoice in the dance, both young men
and old together: for I will turn their mourning into joy,
and will comfort them, and make them rejoice
from their sorrow."*

There are so many ways to rejoice. We rejoice in
praise to God in the singing of songs, the playing of
instruments, the clapping of hands, and the movement of
dance. In Psalm 150, David directs us how to praise the
Lord. Praise him with the trumpet, psaltery, harp, timbrel,
with stringed instruments, organs, loud cymbals, high
sounding cymbals, and the dance. Can you imagine this
beautiful sound and the picturesque setting of rejoicing?

Although many churches presently incorporate dance
into the worship service, dancing while rejoicing also
happened long ago in the Old Testament. David danced
Lord before the Lord when the ark of the Lord was brought
to the city of David. (2 Samuel 6:12-14) David danced to
rejoice before the Lord. Exodus 15:20 states, "And Miriam
the prophetess, the sister of Aaron, took a timbrel in her

hand; and all the women went out after her with timbrels and with dances." The Bible said dancing turned the virgin's heart from sadness into joy. (Jeremiah 31:13)

In our church, (name the dance ministry or ministries) _____Dance Ministry rejoices and praises the Lord in our worship services. We praise God for their ministry. (Firstly, some of us may need stretch and warm up our bones and ligaments before dancing for Jesus.) Dance, O ye people!

Dear Lord, May our feet and our two steps give you praise. We are not sure which dance steps David had in the Old Testament, but our dance steps today is for your glory. Amen.

Songs Related to Rejoice (in the dance):
1. When The Spirit Of the Lord - Fred Hammond
2. Hear Our Praises - Reuben Morgan
3. Dance Like David - Adrian Murley
4. Dance, Dance, Dance - Judith Driver

Mighty

Psalm 24:8

*"Who is this King of glory? The Lord strong and mighty,
the Lord mighty in battle."*

We are in spiritual warfare with the enemy, but our
God is mighty. Our God is mighty in battle. Lift up your
heads! Be strong. Equip yourselves with the armor of God.
Protect your head with the helmet of salvation and hold up
the shield of faith. Girt your loins (groin) with truth and
wear the breastplate of righteousness. Shod your feet with
the preparation of the gospel of peace; and grip the sword
of the Spirit in your hand, which is the Word of God
(Ephesians 6:14-17).

With all of the above, we are not weak in battle. We
are mighty. God has given us the tools to be mighty in
battle. Each piece of our war gear must be put on. Verse 11
states that we must put on the whole amour of God. Do not
leave out any pieces of our armor. We cannot lose! When
we go to battle, we can fight and win!

Dear Lord, When we go to battle, we know you are fighting for us. We know that we wrestle not against flesh and blood, but against principalities. We know we only can win in the strength and power of the Lord. Oh, Lord most holy. We come to you this day. Help us to remember all of the above when we are in battle. Amen.

Songs Related to Mighty:

1. The Battle is Not Yours - V. Michael McKay

2. Lift Up Your Heads Oh Ye Gates (Gospel) -

Preashea Hilliard

3. Lift Up Your Heads (anthem) - Emma L. Ashford

4. When We Go To Battle - Marlene Jenkins Cooper

Cross

Hebrews 12:2

"Looking unto Jesus the author and finisher of our faith;
who for the joy that was set before him endured the cross,
despising the shame, and is set down at the right hand
of the throne of God."

Calvary! Calvary! Jesus paid our debt on Calvary.
How can we repay Him for paying such a price? His blood
poured from His body while on the cross. The pain He
endured can hardly be accurately explained. The payment
for sin was met with His selfless act.

Communion is the one ordinance that we as Christians
follow to remember his death, burial, and resurrection. The
wafer or bread symbolizes Jesus' body, and the wine or
grape juice signifies Jesus' blood. We remember Calvary
when He bore our iniquities. How can we forget the love
He showed for us on Calvary? Amazing love was shed on
Calvary. There is no redemption for us without the cross of
Calvary and the shedding of blood for us by Jesus. Thanks
be to Jesus.

Dear Lord, How can we repay you for the love and act you did on Calvary? We know there is no way to repay you for dying for us on the cross of Calvary. We are free! Praise the Lord; we are free from the penalty of sin and death. Thank you, Jesus! Amen.

Songs Related to Cross:

1. Jesus Keeps Me Near The Cross - Fanny Crosby
                              William Howard Doane

2. Alas, and Did My Savior bleed (At The Cross) -
                    Isaac Watts / Ralph Erskine Hudson

3. I'm Free - Milton Brunson

4. The Old Rugged Cross - George Bennard

Mighty

Psalm 106:2

*"Who can utter the mighty acts of the Lord? who can shew
forth all his praise?"*

There is no one mightier than the Lord our God. He is
mighty in battle and strength. There are multiple examples
of God helping the prophets, kings, and others in the Bible
to be successful. One such example is David during his
battle against Goliath. This was an unfair match (1 Samuel
17). David was unafraid because he knew God would fight
for him.

Each person God helped had to follow His directions
and battle plan. Elijah asking God to send fire under the
altar is an example of the mighty power of God. In 1 Kings
18, God sent the fire from heaven and "consumed the burnt
sacrifice, and the wood, and the stones, and the dust, and
licked up the water that was in the trench" (1 Kings 18:38).
Our God is mighty in battle. Elijah won the fire battle with
the mighty power of God.

God is still mighty in wisdom and strength. What do

you need Him to do for you today? There is no reason why we cannot just stop and praise Him for being mighty in wisdom and strength. Yes, we praise you, Lord God, for your mighty acts, wisdom, and strength.

Dear Lord, God you are strong and mighty.
There is none like you! Amen.

Songs Related to Mighty:

1. Great and Mighty - Marlene Bigley
2. My God is So Big - Ruth Calkin
3. What a Mighty God We Serve - African Folk Song
4. What a Mighty God We Serve - Marcus Dawson

Steven Ford

Voice

Daniel 9:10

"Neither have we obeyed the voice of the Lord our God,
to walk in his laws, which he set before us
by his servants the prophets."

Daniel is speaking the words from today's scripture. Earlier in the chapter, Daniel had expressed his sentiments about the state of affairs with his people. Let us fast-forward 2,000-plus years. Are we listening to the voice of the Lord as a nation, a church, a choir, and as a child of God? The Lord speaks to us through His Word, prayer, scripture meditation and study, circumstances, and sometimes through our sisters and brothers in Christ. Beware when receiving a word from God for you from others. God never contradicts himself. The words of others must line up in agreement with the Word of God.

It's difficult to hear His voice if we do not spend time with Him in prayer and Bible study. Make the time to pray, study, and read the Bible. Some people feel that it is difficult to hear the voice of the Lord. But we have His

Word, the Bible, and He speaks from eternity through His Word.

God always hears us when we pray, but do we hear Him when He speaks? Our circumstances are to teach us lessons that are constructed just for us. Trust and obey God's voice. Hear the voice of the Lord.

Dear Lord, We lift our voices, hands, and sounds from our instruments in praise and adoration and on one accord. We pray we hear your voice when you speak to us individually and as a group. Hear our prayer, O Lord. Amen.

Songs Related to Voice:
1. With a Voice of Singing - Martin Shaw
2. I Heard the Voice of Jesus Say - Horatius Bonar
3. I Heard the Voice of Jesus - Edwin Hawkins
4. Lift Up Your Voice and Sing - James Weldon Johnson
J. Rosamond Johnson

Refuge

Psalm 62:7-8

"7 In God is my salvation and my glory: the rock of my strength, and my refuge, is in God. 8 Trust in him at all times; ye people, pour out your heart before him: God is a refuge for us. Selah."

We can take refuge in the Lord because He promised never to leave or forsake us. God's refuge is shelter from the storms in our lives, protection from dangers seen and unseen, and safety in His arms. We can run to God for anything!

Some people think we only run to Jesus in terrible and stressful times. No, no, no! We also run or maybe walk to Jesus in great times. Our heavenly Father loves us and wants a relationship with us. It is a wonderful experience to talk to the Lord and tell Him everything. God gives us such great strength as He imparts wisdom, guidance, and instructions to us. When God speaks, we should listen to His voice. When we need comfort, hear the words of the Lord. Our refuge and strength is God.

Where you gonna run to? We are running to God for our refuge and strength! God will never leave us alone. When we pass through dark times and deep waters, He promised to be right there with us. Read His Word, pray, and listen. Jesus is the refuge for our souls.

Dear Lord, So glad we can find refuge in you. Where can we flee? We run to you, O Lord. We can hide with you, our refuge and strength. Amen.

Songs Related to Refuge:

1. What A Friend We Have in Jesus (vs. 2) -
   Joseph M. Scriven / Charles C. Converse
2. Refuge For My Soul - Ronald King

3. How Firm a Foundation (vs. 1) - Unknown
4. Jesus, Lover of My Soul - Charles Wesley

Worship

John 4:24

"God is a Spirit: and they that worship him must worship him in spirit and in truth."

When do we worship God the Father? Right now! Anytime. Sunday morning worship service is not the only time we worship God. We also come together to worship our living God during our rehearsals. Worshipping God should also occur in our personal time as well.

In American, we are blessed that we can worship openly without any governmental opposition. There are persons in this world who must go underground to worship Christ as a body of believers. During our worship times together and alone, our hands are sometimes lifted towards heaven. Many times our heads are lifted or bowed in humble submission to Him. There are noisy worshippers as well as quiet ones. God accepts our worship when we worship Him in spirit and in truth. We worship and adore Him. Give Him the honor and glory due Him. Come, let us worship Him!

Dear Lord, You are so worthy of our praise, adoration, and worship. As we sing during this rehearsal and in the sanctuary during our worship services, it is our desire to worship you in spirit and in truth. Please accept our worship. Amen.

Songs of Related to Worship:
1. Worship The Lord - Edwin Hawkins
2. Come Worship the Lord (Beauty of Holiness) -
Nettie L. Lester
3. Come and Let Us Worship - Richard Smallwood
4. We Worship Christ The Lord - James Moore

Battle

2 Chronicles 20:15

"And he said, Hearken ye, all Judah, and ye inhabitants of Jerusalem, and thou king Jehoshaphat, Thus saith the Lord unto you, Be not afraid nor dismayed by reason of this great multitude; for the battle is not yours, but God's."

Can you name any of the groups of people who fought battles with the Israelites in the Old Testament? (Pause.) The Israelites fought different battles with the Philistines, Amalekites, Jebusites, and the Canaanites, just to name a few. Many battles were victorious, but some were lost. One particular battle was won, but the Israelites did not follow God's directive to leave the spoils of the land. They refused to listen to God's instruction.

We sometimes win the battle, but lose the war within ourselves. We need to ask God to help us win the inner wars within ourselves. God will fight our battles if we let Him. Our need to be in control will cause us to take casualties and ultimately lose the battle. Losing is painful. Let go and let God fight for you. Even when you think and are confident that the battle is yours to win on your own, stop! With God on our side, we can fight and win.

Each battle needs to have a plan of attack and a plan for conquering. God has those plans and sees the entire battle before it begins. The first step is to trust God and let Him be the captain of your battle. Take His lead.

Dear Lord, Help! Help us, we pray. We need your direction, power, and foresight as some of us are in the fight of our lives. Victory is on our side. We're trusting in you as we walk through the minefields of life. Please hold our hand and walk us through this battle. Amen.

Songs Related to Battle:

1. The Battle is Not Yours - V. Michael McKay
2. When We Go To Battle - Marlene Jenkins Cooper
3. I am On The Battlefield For My Lord - Sylvana Bell
                                                    E.V. Bank

4. Be Still, God Will Fight Your Battles - Negro Spiritual

Touch

Mark 5:28

"For she said, If I may touch but his clothes,
I shall be whole."

There are so many lessons to be learned from the account of the woman with the issue of blood. (Mark 5:25-34) Lesson 1: She believed Jesus could heal her. She believed that with only a touch from Him she could be made whole. Lesson 2: She acted on her faith and pressed through the crowd to touch him. This woman did not ponder what she should do while Jesus was walking past her. She did not have to be convinced of this fact. She pressed her way to him because she knew that touching Jesus' garment would heal her and make her whole. And she was immediately healed after touching the hem of Jesus' garment. Lesson 3: Just one touch from the Master's hand can heal anything that ails us. The Bible does not state if the woman asked her girlfriends for their opinion of the situation. This woman wanted to be made whole. She pushed her way through the crowd and touched Jesus.

We must believe that Jesus can heal. Many people in the Bible wanted to see the miracles of healing. Jesus healed people with many different ailments and diseases. Need we mention them? Leprosy, blindness, barrenness, paralysis, and crippling diseases, just to name a few. Call to remembrance past healings of friends, family members, and ourselves. Is a healing touch needed today here in this room? Let us pray for God's healing touch. Our faith in the power of Jesus to heal will make us well.

Dear Lord Jesus, touch us! Place your hand on those who are sick in their bodies and need healing. Please heal and intercede for those who need healing in their marriages, home life, schoolwork, and relationships. We are waiting on you. Please touch us, Lord, with your healing hands. Amen.

Songs Related to Touch:
1. He Touched Me - William Gaither / Gloria Gaither
2 Oh It Is Jesus - Andrae Crouch
3. Only A Touch From Jesus - Virginia D. Marshall
                              Anne Shepherd
4. Touch Me Lord Jesus - C. R. Williams
                              Lucie E. Campbell

Free

Romans 8:2

"For the law of the Spirit of life in Christ Jesus hath made me free from the law of sin and death."

Water is free. Air is free. Eternal life is free. Why do people reject salvation when it is free? We need air and water to live. People don't reject the air and water we drink. We need Eternal life to live forever. No one would reject that if they understood!

Although salvation is free, one must freely accept the gift of salvation by taking Christ as their personal Savior. God gives us a choice to believe and accept or reject Him. Salvation frees us from the bondage and penalty of sin and death. As Jesus went around teaching, sharing, doing miracles, and healing, there were those people, notably the Sadducees, Pharisees, publicans, and others, who did not believe Jesus' message and tried to shut Him down and discredit Him with their questioning and accusations. Jesus gave the message of salvation, and one must choose this day whom they will serve.

194

Our music can lead others to Christ, and our lives should reflect the God we serve. It is imperative that our message in song points others to Christ and none other. Prayerfully, our music and testimonies can bring others to the Kingdom.

Dear Lord, Let the words of our music, the tunes of our songs, the text and message of our melodies bring others to Christ. We want others to accept the free gift that we sing about, Jesus Christ. That others may know Him is our prayer. Amen.

Songs Related to Free:
1. I'm Free - Milton Brunson
2. Power In The Blood - Lewis Edgar Jones
3. We Are Free - Morris Chapman
4. Amazing Grace - Chris Tomlin

Light

John 14:6

"Jesus saith unto him, I am the way, the truth, and the life: no man cometh unto the Father, but by me."

Come is a verb that demands an action. Jesus said, "Cometh unto the Father." A person has to make a decision to come to Jesus. After we make the decision, Jesus will save us from our sins. Jesus forces no one to come to Him. It must be an act of individual will. His arms are open for anyone who chooses to come.

Why make the decision? There is a simple, precise, and easily understood answer. Jesus said, "I am the way, the truth, and the life: no man cometh unto the Father, but by me." We cannot have eternal life unless we make the decision to come to him.

There are so many benefits to making the decision. We are walking in darkness if we do not know Jesus as our personal Savior. As soon as someone repents of sin and accepts Christ into their heart, eternal salvation is theirs and the light comes on! Jesus will take all of our burdens and cares, and He gives rest to our weary souls. There is no waiting period—this happens immediately! Come to Jesus! Come to Jesus right now.

(The invitation, plan of salvation, and the Sinner's Prayer begins on page 202.)

Dear Lord, You are the light of life. You brighten the darken path. We pray that our music helps bring people to the light so that they may walk in the light.

Songs Related to Light:

1. Come Unto Jesus (anthem) - Robert Fryson

2. Come Unto Jesus While You Have Time -

Charles H. Nicks Jr.

3. Come To Jesus - Traditional

4. If You Come To Him (Come To Jesus) -

Walter Hawkins

Glory

John 2:11(NIV)

"What Jesus did here in Cana of Galilee was the first
of the signs through which he revealed his glory;
and his disciples believed in him."

In John 2, Jesus performs His first miracle. He turns
the water into fine wine at a wedding feast where the wine
has run out. The disciples believe Him after the miracle.

Really? Do we really need to see a miracle to believe
who Jesus is? Evidently, we do. Jesus turning the water into
wine was the first time He revealed his glory on earth. Do
we need more signs of His glory? I think not. God has
revealed Himself over and over and over. "Jesus I'll Never
Forget" is a song that reminds us what Jesus has done for
us personally and collectively. Jesus still reveals himself to
us individually, to the body of believers, to the church, and
globally. To be in the presence of the Lord and then to sing
about it can be an ethereal experience. He meets us in
worship and prayer. It is His desire for us, each and every
one, to be in relationship with Him.

Oh, the glory of His presence. David spoke about his experience of being in the presence of the Lord in Psalm 16:11. Think about it for a moment. What are your experiences about beholding the glory of the Lord in His presence?

Dear Lord, Oh, the glory of being in Your presence. We honor, worship, and adore you this day. We revere you and extol you. Let our words, songs, and actions be acceptable to you. Please fill this place. We love to be in your presence. In Jesus' name, Amen.

Songs Related to Glory:
1. Oh The Glory of His Presence - Steve Fry
2. The Glory Of The Lord - Richard Smallwood
                         Gloria Gaither / William Gaither
3. The Name of the Lord - Clint Utterbach
4. Let It Rise - Holland Davis

Valley

Luke 3:5 – 6 (NIV)

"Every valley shall be filled in, every mountain and hill made low. The crooked roads shall become straight, the rough ways smooth. And all people will see God's salvation."

Martin Luther King Jr., the civil rights leader, used part of the above verse in his famous "I Have a Dream" speech. Dr. King believed this scripture and lived it. He knew Jesus would "fix it" in His own timing. "It" is social justice, racial equality, great educational experiences for all children, and the abolishment of racism. We as a nation have not arrived, but we are not where we used to be in the 1960s. Some strides have been made in racial equality, but many obstacles still stand in the way.

Jesus had His own valley experience before going to the cross. He couldn't even elicit any of His disciples to pray with Him while agonizing in the garden. Everyone fell asleep. Jesus had to endure alone the knowledge of going to the cross to die and the conspiracy of the people wanting to kill him.

Jesus will walk with us through each of our valley

experiences. A valley experience does not have to be a totally terrible one. God teaches us lessons, strengthens our character, speaks to us, and meets us in the valley. We can leave the valley with memorable lessons and experiences. Crying, loneliness, sadness, and disappointments can be a part of the valley experience. David, the psalmist, wrote about his valley experience in Psalm 23. The Lord met him in the valley, and he was forever grateful.

Dear Lord, We look to you today, the God of the mountains and the valleys. We are grateful you look high and you look low. "You make everything beautiful in your own time." (Ecclesiastes 3:11) As we walk in the valleys and climb the mountains, we look to you to make all things right. We give you thanks. Amen.

Songs Related to the Valley:
1. We Shall Walk Through the Valley of Peace - Arr. Moses Hogan
2. Every Valley - John Ness Beck
3. Ev'ry Valley Shall Be Exalted - George F. Handel
4. Jesus Walked This Lonesome Valley - Folk Song

INVITATION TO SALVATION

If you have sung the words or played the music of the Christian songs in this devotional, or have participated in music ministry in your church or community, but never repented of your sins and asked Christ to save you, you are in need of a Savior. Please consider repenting of your sins, and asking Jesus Christ to save you today. The steps are as easy as A, B, C.

Admit and Repent - Admit you have sinned against GOD and repent of your sins.

What is "sin?"

- Mark 7:21-23 – "For from within, out of the heart of men, proceed evil thoughts, adulteries, fornications, murders, thefts, covetousness, wickedness, deceit, lewdness, an evil eye, blasphemy, pride, foolishness. All these evil things come from within and defile a man."
- James 4:17 – "Therefore, to him who knows to do good and does not do it, to him it is sin."

What is "Admit and repent?"

- Psalm 51:3-4a – "For I acknowledge my transgressions, and my sin is always before me. Against You, You only, have I sinned, and done this evil in Your sight..."
- John 8:11b – "And Jesus said to her, "Neither do I condemn you; go and sin no more."

<u>B</u>elieve and Receive – Believe what the Bible teaches about the Penalty of Sin; that Christ paid the penalty for your sin by His death on the cross, His burial, and His physical resurrection. Receive the gift of His payment in your place.

What is the "Penalty for sin?"

- Ezekiel 18:4 – "Behold, all souls are Mine; The soul of the father as well as the soul of the son is Mine; The soul who sins shall die."
- Romans 6:23 – "For the wages of sin is death, but the gift of God is eternal life in Christ Jesus our Lord."
- Hebrews 9:27 – "And as it is appointed for men to die once, but after this the judgment…"
- Revelation 20:12-15 – "And I saw the dead, small and great, standing before God, and books were opened. And another book was opened, which is the Book of Life. And the dead were judged according to their works, by the things, which were written in the books… Then Death and Hades were cast into the lake of fire. This is the second death. And anyone not found written in the Book of Life was cast into the lake of fire."

What is "His death on the cross, His burial, and His physical resurrection?"

- 1 Corinthians 15:3-5 – "For I delivered to you first of all that which I also received: that Christ died for our sins according to the Scriptures, and that He was buried, and that He rose again the third day according to the Scriptures, and that He was seen by Cephas, then by the twelve."

- Luke 24:39 – "Behold My hands and My feet, that it is I Myself. Handle Me and see, for a spirit does not have flesh and bones as you see I have." When He had said this, He showed them His hands and His feet."

Call and Declare/Confess - Call on the Lord Jesus Christ to save you and Declare publicly that He is your Lord and Master.

- Romans 10:13 – "For "whoever calls on the name of the Lord shall be saved."
- Romans 10:9,10 - "… if you confess with your mouth the Lord Jesus and believe in your heart that God has raised Him from the dead, you will be saved. For with the heart one believes unto righteousness, and with the mouth confession is made unto salvation."

If you sincerely repent of your sins, and believe what the Bible teaches about the penalty of sin (that you want to escape), and Jesus Christ's payment for your sins, by His death on the cross, burial, and resurrection from the dead; if you want Jesus Christ to save you, say the following prayer (or equivalent in your own words):

"Repentant Sinner's Prayer for Salvation"

Dear Lord Jesus Christ,

I admit my sins of thought, word, and deed. I admit that I have sinned against You, and done this evil in Your sight. I am sorry for my sins, and have decided to turn away from all sin. Thank You for dying on the cross to pay the penalty for my sin. Please save me. Please forgive me of all my sins. Please come into my heart and take over as the Lord of my life. I trust your promise that, if I call on your Name, I will be saved. Thank You for saving my soul today!

Amen.

If you prayed the prayer above, (or equivalent in your own words), you have been born again, into God's Family. You are a child of God. What next?

1. Tell someone else, as soon as possible, about the decision you made, and the action you took.
2. God wants you to be sure of the following five things:
   a. Your salvation – 1 John 5:11-13
   b. Your sins have been forgiven, and will be forgiven if you stumble – 1 John 1:9
   c. You can have victory over temptation –
   1 Corinthians 10:13
   d. Your prayers will be answered, as you follow God's conditions – John 16:24
   e. God will guide you in all your decisions –
   Proverbs 3:5,6
3. Get a Bible, read it daily (at least one chapter). Start with the New Testament (Matthew–Revelation), then the Old Testament (Genesis–Malachi). Repeat the process.
4. Find fellowship and be active in a Bible believing, Bible practicing church.

THE AUTHOR

Marlene Jenkins Cooper serves in several music ministries in churches in the Philadelphia area. Additionally, Marlene has served as choral director, worship leader, and vocalist/pianist through music ministries and worship services at various churches throughout the Philadelphia region. Her singing voice has been heard throughout the East Coast, Canada, Caribbean, and Liberia, West Africa. She has also served as a member of a prison ministry, and has applied her professional training to educate children through the Bible and music at various Christian overnight camps and Vacation Bible Schools. She is one of the facilitators for her home church's Where Do I Go From Here? (WDIGFH) ministry, a support group ministry for those who are separated and divorced.

Ms. Cooper's first book, *While in the Valley,* shares ten lessons the author experienced while going through her separation and divorce. God taught her valuable lessons that she draws from daily. *While in the Valley* has ministered to men and women across the United States.

Marlene Jenkins Cooper is also a retired public school teacher from the School District of Philadelphia. During her thirty-four years of service, she not only held the general vocal music teacher position, but later, as computer specialist and music teacher, she taught grades K–8.

Ms. Cooper holds music education degrees from Temple University and The King's College. She is the parent of two adult children, Joy and Mark. She enjoys reading, traveling, cooking, swimming, and playing tennis. Her greatest desire is to bring more people into the Kingdom of God and help people live a victorious Christian life.

DEVOTIONAL THEME INDEX

Adore	98	Devotional Forty-nine
All	66	Devotional Thirty-three
Alone	84	Devotional Forty-two
And They Sang	38	Devotional Nineteen
Angels	54	Devotional Twenty-seven
Anything	146	Devotional Seventy-three
Battle	190	Devotional Ninety-five
Blessings	26	Devotional Thirteen
Blood	96	Devotional Forty-eight
Call	164	Devotional Eighty-two
Care	58	Devotional Twenty-nine
Cast	44	Devotional Twenty-two
Clouds	18	Devotional Nine
Clouds	36	Devotional Eighteen
Communion	126	Devotional Sixty three
Cross	128	Devotional Sixty-four
Calvary	152	Devotional Seventy-six
Cross	180	Devotional Ninety
Crown	110	Devotional Fifty-five
Day	76	Devotional Thirty-eight
Drink / Thirst	90	Devotional Forty-five
Emmanuel	138	Devotional Sixty-nine
Faithfulness	56	Devotional Twenty-eight
Fear	74	Devotional Thirty-seven
Fear Not	72	Devotional Thirty-six
Free	194	Devotional Ninety-seven
Glory	30	Devotional Fifteen
Glory	198	Devotional Ninety-nine
Glory and Honor	32	Devotional Sixteen
Grace	2	Devotional One
Greater	150	Devotional Seventy-five
Hallelujah	28	Devotional Fourteen
Hands	40	Devotional Twenty

Heaven	106	Devotional Fifty-three
Hills	22	Devotional Eleven
Holy	132	Devotional Sixty-six
Hope	92	Devotional Forty-six
Hope	142	Devotional Seventy-one
Jesus	68	Devotional Thirty-four
Joy	52	Devotional Twenty-six
Joy	170	Devotional Eighty-five
King, The	80	Devotional Forty
Knees	16	Devotional Eight
Lamb of God	20	Devotional Ten
Lamp	47	Devotional Forty-seven
Late	50	Devotional Twenty-five
Lift	70	Devotional Thirty-five
Lift	166	Devotional Eighty-three
Light	78	Devotional Thirty-nine
Light	196	Devotional Ninety-eight
Listen	158	Devotional Seventy-nine
Look	34	Devotional Seventeen
Lost	102	Devotional Fifty-one
Love	86	Devotional Forty-three
Love	108	Devotional Fifty-four
Magnify	112	Devotional Fifty-six
Mercy	114	Devotional Fifty-seven
Mighty	100	Devotional Fifty
Mighty	178	Devotional Eighty-nine
Mighty	182	Devotional Ninety-one
Miracle	60	Devotional Thirty
Morning	104	Devotional Fifty-two
Name	174	Devotional Eighty-seven
New	124	Devotional Sixty-two
Nobody	134	Devotional Sixty-seven
Pastures	24	Devotional Twelve
Peace	168	Devotional Eighty-four
Power	46	Devotional Twenty-three
Praise	10	Devotional Five

Praise	64	Devotional Thirty-two
Presence	48	Devotional Twenty-four
Presence	118	Devotional Fifty-nine
Promise	162	Devotional Eighty-one
Ready	88	Devotional Forty-four
Refuge	82	Devotional Forty-one
Refuge	186	Devotional Ninety-three
Rejoice (In the dance)	176	Devotional Eighty-eight
Risen	14	Devotional Seven
Rock	156	Devotional Seventy-eight
Salt	42	Devotional Twenty-one
Satisfy	154	Devotional Seventy-seven
Seek	8	Devotional Four
Serve	116	Devotional Fifty-eight
Shepherd	122	Devotional Sixty-one
Sin	130	Devotional Sixty-five
Sing	12	Devotional Six
Supply	148	Devotional Seventy-four
Teach	140	Devotional Seventy
Temptation	160	Devotional Eighty
Testimony	136	Devotional Sixty-eight
Touch	192	Devotional Ninety-six
Tribulation	62	Devotional Thirty-one
Truth	172	Devotional Eighty-six
Valley	200	Devotional One Hundred
Victory	120	Devotional Sixty
Voice	184	Devotional Ninety-two
Walk	4	Devotional Two
Walk With Me	6	Devotional Three
Wonderful	144	Devotional Seventy-two
Worship	188	Devotional Ninety-four

DEVOTIONAL SCRIPTURE INDEX

Scripture	page #
Genesis	
3:8	118
Deuteronomy	
31:8	72
I Kings	
20:28	22
1 Chronicles	
29:11	98
29:14b	66
2 Chronicles	
20:15	190
29:30	38
Job	
36:5	100
Psalms	
5:3	104
16:11	48
18:1	108
18:3	164
23:1	122
23:2	24
23:4	4
24:8	178
27:1	74
31:24	142
34:3	112
39:7	92

Scripture	page #
46:1	82
62:7-8	186
67:5	10
71:23	170
91:16	154
95:1	156
100:2	116
106:2	182
118:24	76
119:31	136
119:105	94
121:1-2	70
149:1	12
Proverbs	
1:5	158
Isaiah	
6:3	132
9:6	144
26:3	168
Jeremiah	
31:13	176
32:27	146
Lamentations	
3:41	40
Daniel	
9:10	184

Matthew		Romans	
1:23	138	1:16	46
5:13	42	8:2	194
5:16	78		
6:33-34	8	**1 Corinthians**	
28:5-6	14	1:9	56
Mark		10:13	160
4:38	58	15:57	120
5:28	192		
14:22	126	**2 Corinthians**	
		1:20	162
Luke		4:1	114
2:10	54	4:3-4	102
3:5-6	200	5:7	6
12:40	88	5:17	124
21:13	136	5:21	130
23:2-3	80	12:9	2
23:33	152	12:11 (NASB)	134
John		**Galatians**	
1:29	20	5:23-24	52
2:11 (NIV)	198		
3:16	86	**Ephesians**	
4:24	188	1:3	26
6:35	90	3:14	16
8:2	140		
8:32	172	**Philippians**	
11:21	50	2:8	128
12:28	30	2:10-11	68
12:32	166	4:19	148
12:37	60		
12:43	64	**1 Thessalonians**	
14:2-3	106	4:16-17	18
14:6	196		
16:33	62		

Titus

2:13	34

Hebrews

12:2	180
13:5	84

1 Peter

1:7	32
5:4	110
5:7	44

1 John

1:7	96
4:4	150

Revelation

1:7	36
2:17	174
19:1	28

Made in the USA
Monee, IL
28 November 2025

36569942R20134